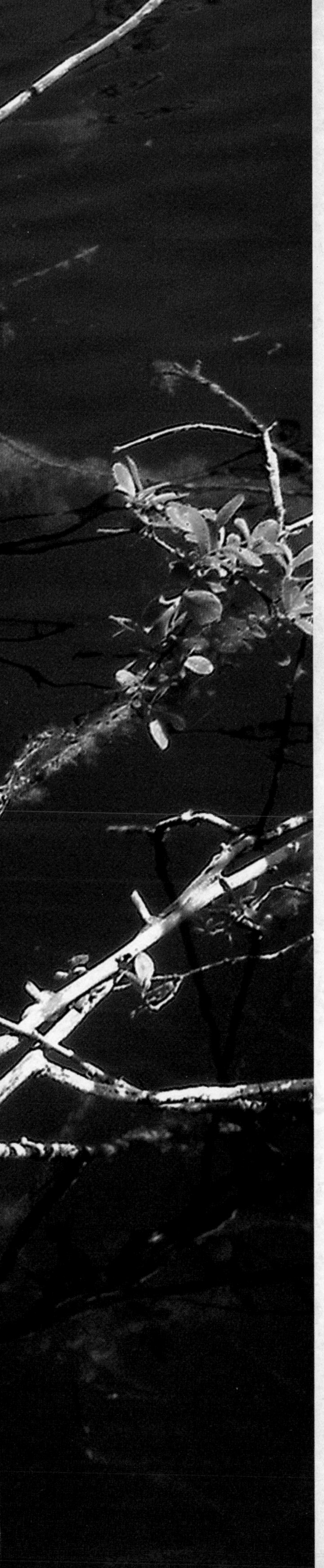

Contents

A Carper's Dozen

A Carper's Dozen

First edition

Published by David Hall Publishing Ltd.
Edited by Marc Coulson
Layout & design by Gary Hood and James Roff
Reprographics by Derek Mooney, Peter Holmes and Thomas Webb

Editorial by Marc Coulson

I had an idea to print the first few words of each angler's reaction when I initially asked them to come up with their favourite carp fishing memories. However, all but one would have been unprintable. The one, by the way, was a stunned silence. I guess that wouldn't have made particularly good reading either!

It's a daunting prospect, especially for the anglers concerned, as each one has, I am sure, a million and one tales that would have been suitable.

I managed to elaborate and explain that I was not looking just for the tale of their biggest carp capture. Nor, necessarily, did I require an account of their most successful session. What I really wanted was a story that they would enjoy telling and that the reader would enjoy reading. After all, that is what a book should surely be about.

The result, after a period of some contemplation, was the wonderful collection of carp fishing exploits that you now hold in your hands.

When 13 of the country's leading carp catchers, including former record holders, captors of huge foreign and English carp and writers of high repute, are gathered together, the result is always going to be something to treasure. I can say, with my hand placed firmly on my heart, that this is indeed a special publication. I am privileged to have worked with each of the anglers concerned, as well as to be able to put my name alongside them in A Carper's Dozen. I offer no apology in stating how highly I regard this collection and I know you will understand my enthusiasm when you read it for yourselves.

Each tale has a style of its own, an individual slant and a unique atmosphere. Reading through every one of the 13 accounts had me captivated and I am sure they will leave you equally aghast.

From Dave Lane's exploits chasing a single, perhaps-record carp in the vast Sonning, to Steve Renyard's and Frank Warwick's big hits, each takes the reader on a journey through a memorable session, campaign or capture. Lee Jackson has become one of carp fishing's favourite writers and he and fellow Kent ace Paul Forward has each penned fascinating and humorous stories.

The impressive Gareth Fareham writes his piece on northern carp Mecca, Redesmere, with such an imaginative style that I genuinely felt as though I'd been there with him. My great friend Neil Smith also tells his tale from the northwest of England. This time it's an atmospheric estate lake, so typical of the region, with some mystical carp lurking in its murky depths.

Jim Shelley takes Horton Church Lake apart on surface baits, Richard Farnan ventures to a virgin carp water of genuine unknown quantity and Dave Levy and Colin Davidson each tempt impressive fish from their home county of Essex.

All of this – along with Adam Penning's tale of his campaign on the ultra-difficult Elstow 2, and the inimitable Derek Ritchie recounting a century of 20lb carp in one season – help make A Carper's Dozen a compendium of some of the finest carp fishing tales ever told.

I am particularly pleased that each writer has not necessarily chosen his biggest-ever carp for his memorable tale. I am sure you all have favourite memories of your own, and again they won't necessarily include your biggest captures. Mine certainly don't. In fact, my favourite comes from the stunning Hunt's Corner lake in Oxfordshire and only includes a couple of 20lb-plus carp.

I am always discussing with fellow anglers the fact that carp don't have to be big to be impressive and worth catching.

These two fish were particularly treasured captures, not least because they were from such a stunning water and in the middle of winter.

"So, our favourite fishing tales are not always the ones about our biggest carp. Indeed, one or two of mine do not include any fish to my rods at all."

I fished Hunt's Corner for a series of features in Total Carp magazine, along with top Midlands' carper Mark Law. It wasn't long before I fell in love with the place and the venue was as much to blame as the fish that swim in it. You see, sometimes it really can be just about being there, regardless of how many you catch or how big they are.

After catching our share of the small stockies, I really wanted to catch one of the originals, especially at this particular time of year, when they would be resplendent in their winter colours.

The first original came on my third trip and was a low twenty with a lovely scale pattern – a kind of 'broken linear' as I referred to it at the time. I was thrilled and went on to share a few more originals with Mark. Then, on a chilly February morning, we'd had a long conversation with Colin the bailiff about the lake. I was keen to find out as much as possible about the stock and wanted to know how many commons or mirrors we were fishing for. He spoke of all the usual targets, from humpy-backed commons to huge, plated mirrors. Then he mentioned 'the leather', almost as an afterthought in fact.

Mark and I both commented that we'd like to catch that one, despite Colin telling us that it was far from being the biggest in the pond. I love genuine leather carp. Their fins seem to melt into their scaleless flanks. I'd only ever caught one genuine leather before, back in my match fishing days, at little over double figures. I also took a perverse pleasure from the fact that this Hunt's Corner leather was the only one of it's kind in the lake and so would be a very worthy capture.

Colin left us, and my thoughts drifted to that fish for the rest of the day. An hour or so before packing-up time, and without a fish so far that day, I saw one head and shoulder in the far margin. I cast out a single pop-up where I'd seen the carp and then sat back and dreamed of the leather snaffling my hook bait.

You may have already guessed, as there are a strange number of these 'coincidences' in carp fishing, that the rod soon rattled off and I landed the stunning leather at 23lb 10oz.

Mark couldn't believe it, as we'd only spoken about it earlier, but I was not at all surprised. That might sound strange, but I'd fantasised about catching it and now firmly believed in my ability to 'will' my next capture on to the bank. This was how I'd read it in so many stories before, so surely there was something in it. There are similar accounts in this very book. Alas, it has never happened to me since, although not for the want of trying. It does not matter though, as the capture of that leather will stay with me forever.

So, our favourite fishing tales are not always the ones about the biggest fish. Indeed, one or two of mine do not include any fish to my rods at all. Whatever else they may be, they are all special – that's what makes the memories fond ones.

Enjoy reading A Carper's Dozen and enjoy each wonderful story in its own individual way. Most of all though, enjoy your own carp fishing experiences and cherish every one of them for as long as you tread the banks, and beyond.

Tight lines and all that…

Thank You!

It would be wrong to publish a book of this nature without first of all thanking those who have made it possible.

To Gary Hood and James Roff, two highly talented designers, for the layout of this wonderful publication and to the 13 anglers that gave us the material to do so. To our sub editor, Lee Jones, for his efforts in making our writings legible; the DHP reprographics department for doing likewise with all the prints and transparencies that were provided; Jon Bones for helping out with a few last-minute hitches and, finally, to my wife Sharon for putting up with the late nights and early mornings in order to get it out on time.

An Obsession With The Long One

Lee Jackson reflects on a session that saw him drive untold miles, fish in two different counties and land a stunning target fish...

By today's standards, the following catch might be deemed nothing out of the ordinary, such is the way that carp weights have drastically increased and the ability that has been gained by some of our modern-day carp anglers at making such catches. Even so, considering the length of session and the effort put in to achieving such a catch, there can't be too many modern-day whizz kids that wouldn't be pleased to have made it, even nowadays.

Firstly, because the main water featured in this story has a no-publicity rule, you'll have to forgive me for just referring to it as the private Hertfordshire club water, as I still relish keeping my permit to fish there.

In a round about way I suppose you could say that this story starts during January 1993 and then ends two years later in October 1995. Anyone that knows me will know that I have always had the philosophy of trying to catch as many carp as I can and then hoping that one or two big ones grace my landing net along the way. Apart from She and then Two Tone, both of which ultimately took me a lot of years to capture, I've never really had an obsession for catching any particular carp. I'd hoped to, maybe, but I'd never really been obsessed as I was with those two. Having said that, the events of a particular January session back in 1993, very nearly saw me obsessed, at catching another particular carp, a magnificent-looking beast being cradled in the arms of my fishing pal Martin Locke (Lockey). This was perhaps the most impressive and best-looking carp that I had ever laid eyes on at the time. I had fished the Herts club water on and off since first joining it in 1983 and caught its first-ever forty at 40lb 4oz, an absolutely immense carp for this time.

Now then, where are you, carp?

Difficult Water

Although fishing on this water couldn't be deemed difficult by Conningbrook or maybe Wraysbury standards, because of the distance from home and not being able to night fish, it had a whole set of difficulties of its own to contend with. For a start, if you wanted to do a two-day session, it meant either packing up at 10.30pm and then spending an uncomfortable night of sleeping in the car, or braving the M25 or London traffic and driving home, only to have to be getting up at 2am to drive back again! Whatever, it was, and remains, quite a difficult water to fish if you lived a long way away and required a lot of determination and effort in order to succeed. It's a far cry from curling up in your sleeping bag and going to sleep on the banks of Conningbrook or Wraysbury and then hoping for it to happen! Another thing on this water was that, seemingly, no two days were ever alike, and if you were lucky enough to catch or be on fish on the first day, the next it would seem like being on a completely different water. Like a lot of waters, winter was usually a complete waste of time. Four months of fishing and only the odd little window of opportunity – not much use if you've got a full-time job, a wife, kids and everything else that goes with it.

The winter of 1992/93 and Lockey had been able to make the most of the little windows of opportunity and had been consistently catching to the extent of being ultra-confident and ultra-successful on this normally difficult winter water. The swim chosen by Lockey for his winter assault was known as The Lawn, a swim with a bit of a track record for producing at this time of year, albeit in all probability due to it being the most consistently fished swim. Out in front of this swim were seven gravel bars, all running fairly parallel to the bank and at a distance of about 10 yards apart. Beyond the seventh bar was a fairly large area of silt, and it was my guess that the carp would be laid up in this area and then venture in towards the bars on the rare occasions that they were willing to feed.

> **"Lockey had been able to make the most of the windows of opportunity and had been consistently catching and was now ultra-confident."**

Pole Position

I arrived on the Thursday morning to find Lockey already set-up in pole position (like he would be), and no doubt with his two rods cast in the hotspot area on or around the seventh bar. In normal circumstances, anglers would double-up in this swim, as it was plenty big enough and there is enough scope to cast four rods. Although we are mates, and I was dropping a few subtle hints, it was obvious that Lockey wasn't go to back down and offer to let me share his swim. Understandable I suppose, due to his recent successes. The fact was that you had to make the most of it if you were catching them in winter on this water. Even though there were a few better options, as another swim known as The 29 had also been producing a few fish recently, I decided to go into the swim next to Lockey, a swim I'd named The 12 o'clock Lawn back in 1984. At least then we could have a bit of a chat and share a few cups of tea. Another reason for going in next to Lockey was that there might just have been a chance of sneaking a rod round in his direction should an opportunity arise – no chance! He'd obviously worked out my intentions, therefore never ventured out of his swim and watched my every move like a hawk. I should have known, he was another Kent boy, so was well wised-up to stroke-pulling or mind games!

Dominant Bait

All of Lockey's recent captures, which had included a 40, and a 38, as well as a few other good fish, had fallen for pop-ups made from his own Squid & Octopus mix. This was to form the basis of the yet-to-be-developed Club Mix, a bait that was to dominate catches on this water, plus many others, in years to follow. I must admit I didn't quite share Lockey's confidence at using bait containing fishmeal in winter. That said, used as high-attract single hook baits, they can be devastatingly effective, as Lockey's catches were proving.

As the day wore on, the weather conditions were improving all the time, as we could feel the drop in air pressure and the southwesterly wind was increasing all the time. Over the many years that I have winter fished for carp, I have developed a distinct liking for two particular contrasting types of weather systems. For one, I like days with a frosty start that develop into a bright sunny day with flat-calm conditions. The other is low cloud, low pressure, winds from a south or westerly direction and a bit of drizzly rain.

By darkness the conditions looked bang-on and, although there hadn't been any fish sightings, it was no surprise when one of Lockey's rods went rattling off. Initially there were a few tense moments as the fish hugged the back of the bar and his main line went grating along the top. The bars on this lake had always been a bit of a problem. In fact, in the early days of fishing on there, when we used significantly finer main lines to what is normally used nowadays, it wasn't uncommon to get cut-off even before you had time to strike. Even if you didn't get cut-off, your line would be coming in severely frayed, causing much anxiety until the fish was finally netted.

Scream Of Delight

Eventually, and after the fish had snagged-up a couple of more times on the closer-in bars, it was at last chugging up and down the margins and would soon be Lockey's, save any strokes of ultra-bad luck. Because of the now quite strong wind, the rain and the fact that it was dark, I crouched down low with the landing net, as it was quite difficult to see. I'm never nervous about netting my own fish but terrified of making a cock-up of netting somebody else's, especially so when you know it's a big 'un. A few more lunges for freedom and eventually it was wallowing on its side and ready to be netted. As I engulfed it in the folds of the net, Lockey let out a scream of delight, spurred on by my exclamation that it was most definitely a forty.

We carp anglers are so privileged to have views like this from our bivvies.

> **"Lockey ran to get the camera and scales. I reeled in one of my rods as quickly as I could and cast it into his swim – what me, stroke pull?"**

Folding back the mesh to inspect the prize, our breath was taken away. It was an absolutely stunning and immaculate-looking carp known as The Long One and one of the biggest carp in the lake. While leaving me to secure the fish in a sack, Lockey ran off to fetch his camera and scales from his van. This was too good an opportunity for me to miss, so, with the fish safely sacked up in the edge, I reeled in one of my rods as quickly as I could and then cast it over into Lockey's swim – what me, stroke pull? Never!

Just when I was tidying the swim, this rod roared off, taking me more than a bit by surprise. Straightaway I knew that it wasn't a big one, therefore a little thought of devilment set in. If I could get this carp in and sacked up before Lockey's return, when it came to getting his fish out for weighing and photographing, I'd get this one out instead – imagine his confusion! Well had it not been for the fact that I'd never before set up a Solar Bow Loc landing net, and was struggling to do so, it would've very nearly worked. Unfortunately, Lockey returned before I could net the fish. "What, you got one as well Jacko?" "Yes mate, on my right-hand rod that's been out there all day!"

One Day Jacko

Lockey's carp weighed 41lb 3oz and mine 27lb 12oz. While squatting down next to each other and posing for a double photo, I couldn't take my eyes off Lockey's carp; it was that impressive – one day Jacko, one day. Although I wasn't set to becoming obsessed at catching this carp, it would certainly enter my mind regularly and is one that I hoped to make the acquaintance of at some time in the future – and the sooner the better.

A couple of years down the line and we'd really established our bait to the extent that we were enjoying the lion's share of the catches on the Herts club water. Predominantly, the Solar Club Mix had been the brainchild of Paul Forward ('F'), although each of us had a hand in designing the attractor combination, which culminated in around 200ml of natural liquid attraction being added to 1kg of base mix. There was no doubt about it, 'F', Alun Parsons, 'Secret' Steve Curtin, Lockey and myself had worked as a team and had got 'our' bait established to the extent that the carp were viewing it as a natural food and searching it out as a preferable food source.

Throughout the summer months we caught fish on a fairly regular basis and I think 'F', Steve and Alun all managed to catch personal bests, all a few pounds in excess of the 40lb barrier.

What had always been very important on this lake was to try to find the feeding spots, in fact more so than any other lake that I had fished before, or indeed since. Because of the vast amount of gravel bars and features that this lake contains, it was never quite enough to cast to a rolling or leaping fish, you needed to be bang on the money and on the spot where it fed, instead of just in the vicinity. I used to imagine the topography of the lake bed as being made up of silt areas, large boulder-type stones, smaller stones and occasional small spots where the smaller stones felt 'polished' and therefore fed on. On most occasions that I fished the lake I would spend quite a bit of time frantically casting around with a marker/feature-finding set-up, trying to find a 'polished' spot to present my bait on and therefore be very confident of getting a bite. I've got to admit that on the majority of occasions I would often get fed up of searching after about 20 or so casts and would settle for fishing spots that didn't 'feel' too bad. This, though, was never really quite good enough and usually resulted in a blank.

One particular Thursday during the autumn of this year I was in a swim called Dorton's, my favourite swim on the lake and a swim that I knew reasonably well. At this time of year the hot period had always been evenings, and in particular the last hour before you had to pack up at 10.30pm. Because of this, it never used to bother me a great deal about disturbing the swim and having a cast around in order to find spots. As long as the baits were in good positions by darkness, that was all that really mattered. During the day I found two prime spots, albeit only very small ones, with the marker float rod that I'd got loaded up with braid. At the time, braid was a fairly new discovery for feature finding and 'feeling' the bottom and the extra sensitivity that it gave made it a great deal easier to find spots and learn the topography of the lake bed. The trouble was, I could only find these spots with the marker rod. I couldn't feel them at all with my main fishing rods loaded with ordinary monofilament. Then I had a bit of a brainwave. Why not try fishing with braid as main line, at least then I would know that my baits were presented on the right spot. With that thought, I bit off my main line about 20 feet above my end tackle and then attached it to the braid on the marker rod. This was more like it; it almost felt as though I was running my hand across the lake bed! Although nothing happened that particular session, I baited both spots with around 200 boilies before I left and vowed to change the other rod over to braid before my return trip the following Thursday.

My wife had a disbelieveing look that said: "You're mad, going to drive 76 miles for three hours' fishing and then back again?"

Chores Completed

Sunday afternoon soon came and, with most of my household chores completed, it was time to start thinking about going out fishing for the evening. In normal circumstances I would fish reasonably close to home for an evening, but as I only had one swim and two spots in mind, I knew where I was heading. I said my goodbyes to my wife, who had that disbelieving look on her face that said: "You're mad, you're going to drive

This made me one very happy carp angler.

76 miles for about three hours' fishing and then drive 76 miles back again!" All the way up there I was hoping and praying that there would be nobody occupying the swim. If there was, then I might just as well turn straight round and drive back again. Two hours later I arrived at the car park to find eight cars and my heart sank. There was a very good chance that Dorton's would be occupied because it's quite a popular swim. Sprinting along the bank with the barrow, I was counting the other anglers as I went - one, two, three, four, five, six, seven - sod it, only one angler to find now, Bob Copeland, and I bet that he's in there. Eventually my spirits were lifted, Bob was in The Gravelly so there was no need to rush now, as Dorton's was mine. We exchanged the usual pleasantries and I listened to Bob's very amusing version of the English language. As anyone that knows Bob will tell you, he's got a version all of his own that's a sort of cross between cockney, gypsy, West Indian and Middlesex. "How's it going then tiger, you alright then son, how's the wife and the chavvy's son, are they alright then son?" "Go and get yerself sorted out then son, I'll be along for a cup of rosy in a bit." "Your alright then are you tiger, I'll see you in a while!"

I pushed along to Dorton's and then thought - I'll be alright in a minute tiger, at least I will when I've got these two baits out on the money I will!

In normal circumstances it would take quite a while to get my baits in position to my liking. Not this time though, first cast with the left-hand rod and I could easily feel the polished stones as I drew my lead along the lake bed on the 90-yard spot. It was the same with the right-hand rod, except this spot was only about 70 yards out. I was mightily impressed with the braid, not only because of the ease of finding the spots, but also its casting properties. It absolutely sailed out there with virtually no noise caused by it rattling through the rings. I put out about 50 or so free offerings around each rod and then sat back for a well-earned brew. To say I was confident was an understatement; I knew that I was going to get a bite; it was just a case of when.

Carp Chat

About an hour into darkness, Bob popped along for a chat and the cup of tea that I had promised him. We chatted about this and that and I told Bob about my changeover to using braid as main line and the advantages that it seemed to offer. As well as bait presentation and casting advantages, I also felt that because of its near-zero-stretch characteristics, it might also offer better and more positive bite indication, especially so if it was fished as a tight line. One thing I didn't know was what it would be like to play fish on… yet.

As the evening wore on, so my expectations grew, because the nearer it got to 10.30, so the chances of a bite would improve. Fairly soon the subject of conversation turned to which of the lake's residents we would most like to catch. Although this lake contained quite a few sought-after carp, such as Chop Dorsal, Dearman's, Dearman's Mate, Tyson, plus quite a few others, for me there was really no doubt

> **"I don't really care what carp I catch but if I had to choose it would undoubtedly be The Long One."**

as to which one I'd most like to catch and my mind drifted back to Lockey in The Lawn swim a couple of years previous. Without wishing to sound blasé, I'd caught most of the big fish in there, so turned to Bob and said: "I'll tell you what mate, I don't really care what carp I catch from this lake, the bigger the better obviously, but if I had to choose just one it would undoubtedly be The Long One!" With that my mind drifted off into visions of a perfectly proportioned carp with chestnut-coloured flanks and more muscles

The picture says it all!

han Arnold Schwarzenegger. I must have been night dreaming' for about two minutes when he 90-yard rod went into absolute overdrive vith a bite so fast that I was almost scared to ›ick up the rod. It was at this point that I now vasn't quite so sure about using the braid, as vhatever it was that I had on the other end vas trying to pull my arm out of its socket! It vas obvious straightaway that this was a very ›ig fish and playing on braid was proving a bit iairy. A couple of times during the fight I felt he sickening sensation of my line pinging icross its dorsal fin, which on nylon is bad :nough, but on braid it nearly caused me a :ardiac arrest. What wasn't making things any ›etter were Bob's words of reassurance: "Take t easy tiger, this is a really big fish, you've iearly got it beaten, don't want to go and lose t now do you son!" After what seemed like an ıbsolute age, a great big, long flank came vallowing to the surface and Bob crouched lown with the net and very expertly netted it irst time of asking. Bob was the first one in vith the torch and straightaway said: "You've ;ot it son, it's The Long One!" I was lost for vords and didn't know whether to scream ›ut loud, do somersaults or give Bob a great ›ig kiss. We did the usual thing with the ınhooking mat and so on, and then hoisted he scales – 46lb 4oz and a new personal best. \s I held the fish for the photos and admired ts beauty, I couldn't help thinking how lucky 'd been. I'd only been looking at this fish in ny dreams a short while ago and here it now vas in my arms, I was ecstatic.

Fish On!

Recasting the rod was proving difficult ›ecause I still had the shakes and therefore :ouldn't quite manage to get it back out on he same spot. Never mind though, I was appy and contented to have caught what I ıad and still had one rod left out there on a ;ood spot. About half an hour later and the ılarm on the right-hand rod gave a few beeps ınd the bobbin started to tremble. I can emember asking Bob if he thought this was a ›ite and then striking before he me gave an ınswer. It was a bite all right and another carp ugged and thrashed on the end of the braid, ılbeit not quite as ferociously as the previous ›ne had done. Again the braid gave a few ınxious moments, although I was a little bit nore laid back about playing this one and :onfident that everything would hold out. As ›efore, Bob did an expert job with the net and ınother good fish was hoisted onto the still-vet unhooking mat. I'd caught this carp ›efore at 19lb quite a few years previously, :asily recognisable by the large scales on its houlders. Well now it was quite a bit bigger han 19lb, 13lb 12oz bigger in fact, at 32lb 2oz. I turned to Bob and said: "How about hat then tiger, not a bad evening's fishing!"

Certainly better than being at work!

Fairly soon it was time to reel in the rods, make the long walk back to the car, and then negotiate the long drive home, although the way I felt I could've carried Bob's gear as well, and floated all the way.

With the car stereo pumping out full blast and me trying to do my best at imitating the voice of Led Zeppelin's Robert Plant, I had loads of time to reflect on my success. Not only was I very pleased with what I had just caught, I was also very pleased at the performance of the braid and it was obvious that it would give an advantage and a bit of an edge in the future. What was also obvious was that there was no way that I was going to be able to sleep once I got home, as I felt as hyperactive as a kid on orange squash. I pulled off the motorway at the South Mimms services and rang my wife, telling her what I had caught and that I was going to cast my rods out at Cotton Farm and chill out for the rest of the night. In all probability, and from the tone of her voice, she probably didn't give a monkey's what I had just caught and was thankful of getting a good night's sleep without having to put up with my snoring.

I arrived at Cotton a little after midnight, and with sixth-sense fish location, got myself set up on the Small Beach. In comparison to where I'd just come from, casting out at Cotton during darkness was relatively easy due to the lights from the surrounding offices. Unlike the Herts club water, three rods are allowed on Cotton, although rather than rig up another one, I decided just to fish with two, so cast one across to the reeds in Farmhouse Corner and the other out to the fountain. Like you do, because of my success in Hertfordshire, I decided to employ similar tactics of 20mm straightforward bottom baits, a moderate amount of free offerings around each and then fish with the braid as tight as I could possibly get it. I sat back, opened a can of beer and then marvelled at the strange Cotton atmosphere.

By day, Cotton is a hustle and bustle place with office workers going about their daily business, vehicles toing and froing from the car parks, the constant hum of traffic coming across the Dartford Bridge and the distant sounds of police or ambulance sirens. By night though, the place has an almost eerie tranquillity that is only very occasionally disturbed by prowling foxes, the clicking of bat wings and the occasional crash of a night-feeding carp. I shivered as an unsuspecting creature let out a shrill as it was murdered. Just then another shrill rang out, only this time from the bite alarm on the left-hand rod. The braid made easy work of subduing a small common of around 12lb. I replenished the hook bait, recast to the corner, and then climbed into the sleeping bag to try to get some sleep, which although hard to find, was very necessary, as I had to be at work in just a few hours' time.

Last Knockings

My body clock stirred me from my sleep at around first light but there was confusion, as I couldn't shake a buzzing sound from my head. I sat up on the bedchair, swung my legs around to the side and then stared at the right-hand rod that was absolutely blitzing out – here we go again! Instead of charging around like a mad thing, this one stayed deep and held its own. It was obviously one of the better fish in the lake. After about five minutes it was wallowing on its side and ready to be netted and I pinched myself to make sure that I wasn't dreaming as it slipped into the landing net. Indeed, it was one of the biggest fish in the lake at the time, an old English warrior of 29lb 12oz. What a session, 13 hours fishing on two waters, in two different counties. I got into work and was asked how I'd got on: "Oh not bad, I had a 46, a 32, a 29 and a little one of about 12lb." – I pinched myself again!

A Carp For

All Seasons

Steve Renyard tells how his all-year-round approach brought him some fantastic success at a stunning Berkshire water...

Angling for carp is, for some, a spring and summer event, but for many others, including myself, carp fishing is a 12 months of the year quest, whatever the weather. I just love being out there carp fishing – and have done for many, many years.

My main target water over the last few years has been a mature 35-acre gravel syndicate pit in Berkshire. I have met many anglers on this water, some have a few target fish to catch and leave once they achieve their goal and others just enjoy what is in front of them.

I am an old romantic when it comes to carp angling. Once I'm latched onto a venue, I find it really hard to let go.

For example, I was once a member of the original Withy Pool syndicate. This place was in my blood. In fact, I was in the syndicate for nine years before the owner changed it to day ticket. It was an awesome lake, but I suppose he did me a favour really, helping me to make the decision to move on. I was fishing other waters but they didn't float my boat like Withy did.

A few years later I stumbled upon my latest obsession, the Berkshire lake. To this day, nobody knows exactly how many carp inhabit the lake, but we estimate it to be about 200.

Many of the fish are over 20lb, with a good head of thirties. Being selective for bigger carp is my main interest; it's where I get my buzz, and I am constantly trying new methods and theories aimed at landing them. However, it has to be said, I don't mind catching carp of any size – whether they are 14lb or 40lb.

Springtime

Spring is my favorite time of year, both generally and on the Berkshire pit. The trees start budding, you start to see a lot more wildlife, and more importantly the carp tend to become more active.

After a normal British winter, which is usually pretty harsh (though our winters seem to be getting warmer due to global warming) carp seek warmer days and plenty of food to replenish the fat supplies used throughout the colder months.

So there I was, one particular early spring session, with three nights ahead of me, wondering what each might bring.

It was mid-April and not particularly warm but I soldiered on, like you do. My plan was to have a big baited area for two rods and be a bit subtler with my third.

I opted to spod a large area of hemp and crushed tiger nuts, mixed with Grubber pellets. I really wanted to give them a variety of small baits to hold them in my area for as long as possible. Over the top of this, I put 3kg of Richworth's Crab & Mussel boilies, in varying sizes.

Sunrise on the Berkshire lake – often a prolific time on there.

> **"To this day nobody knows exactly how many carp inhabit the lake, but we estimate it to be about 200, many of which are over the 20lb barrier, with a good head of thirties to boot."**

This helps to confuse the carp when they are sucking up bait because they have to use differing amounts of effort when sucking for different sizes of boilies, making the hook bait harder to detect.

To gauge which method would work best on the bid area, I used a pop-up on one rod and a bottom bait on another. The other rod was fished with just boilies and on a bottom-bait rig.

Excited, I sat there ready for the night ahead. I couldn't have been asleep for more than an hour when the first run came. What a screamer it was too!

A frantic battle ended with a huge carp being slipped into my waiting net. She really let me know who was boss when I was fighting her, so I was pleased to get her on the mat.

What a start that was to the year, a magnificent 34lb 10oz common. I recast the rod back on the spot first time. I would hazard a guess that not even an hour had passed before I was involved in another good battle.

I got the impression that this was a much smaller fish, but I was wrong. It was a lovely mirror that managed to pull the scales round to 31lb 8oz. This was the stuff that dreams are made of, I thought. Two thirties in little more than 45 minutes!

The action continued with a wonderful 27lb common. At first light the big baited area really started to pay dividends and I had a succession of big fish, mostly over 24lb.

By this time my tally was getting pretty serious. Due to the fact that I had enjoyed so much action, I decided to re-spod the main area of food, ready for the night ahead. Yet again I didn't have to wait long until I hooked a fish.

The next take was a very slow one. As I lifted the rod I felt solid resistance, with the odd delicate but powerful lunge. I knew that I was into something special. She plodded around very slowly, occasionally taking 10 to 15 yards of line.

Being an old romantic, I felt it was a perfect moment. The moon was shimmering above, with a gentle breeze on the water. It was a carp fishing heaven that was made even better when I got the huge mirror in the folds of my net.

I slowly and carefully hoisted her onto my unhooking mat to reveal my capture. On the scales, she pulled the magic needle round to

The carp I have managed to catch have been varied and each one has offered me lots of satisfaction. From big mirrors abroad, stunningly coloured carp in the UK and a fair few commons thrown in for good measure, I have been lucky to catch many stunning fish. Long may it continue.

39lb 2oz. This was an amazing session but, like a greedy pig, I yearned for more.

A couple of hours passed and I was still wide awake – adrenaline pumping through my entire body. Then the same rod was away again – blimey, what was this all about!

This time the fish was not very happy with the situation. It stripped at least 70 yards of line from my Baitrunner on the initial run. I had only ever had catfish do that to me before, and there were none of them in here.

After 15 minutes the carp was safely in my net – another thirty, at 34lb 8oz. This was certainly not to be sniffed at. I'd now had four thirties and 14 other fish over 24lb in the session, and I still had one night to go! Was it possible that I could get another?

I wasn't sure. After all, I had run out of my incredible spod mix that had done the damage, so I topped up the area with some more Crab & Mussel boilies. In fact, I baited up with all the boilies I had left, leaving a few hook baits. The fish liked the bait so much that it didn't bother me at all just using boilies.

The last night didn't disappoint either. I had a take at 2am that turned out to be a fantastic 29lb 8oz starburst, red-coloured mirror. If you look at the photograph I think you will agree that is a stunning fish.

An hour later I had another take, which really gave me the runaround. It turned out to be another mirror and, weighing in at 33lb 6oz, she truly capped off a memorable trip.

I'm sure by now you can see why I like spring so much. The total fish count was five thirties, 15 between 24lb and 30lb and two upper doubles. Amazing! It was the best session of that spring and one that'll stay with me forever.

Summer Breeze

Another fabulous capture came down at the Berkshire pit during the following summer; one that proves there's more to this carp fishing lark than sitting behind three buzzers.

I love overnighters during summer because some days are just too hot for me to bear. The night offers a respite and a good chance of a carp or two.

Fishing for carp in high summer, in the months of July and August in particuler, can be a bit hit or miss. Our beloved creatures become preoccupied with the rituals of spawning and feeding on the vast supplies of natural food that abound in lakes at this time of year. Summertime is ideal for stalking because carp get into places they don't normally visit at other times of the year.

I had one particular overnighter where I spodded some hemp and corn first for my main rods, then wanted to rest my swim and decided to go for a stalking session. I found a few bubblers in a tiny bay at one end of the lake. Being of the calm, cool type, I legged it, frantically, back to get a rod and some bait! They were still bubbling when I got back so I lowered my rig in very quietly, put a few boilies in and sat behind a bush. I only had to wait 10 minutes before I could hear the Baitrunner churning away. When I looked out I could see a mass of bubbles that the hooked fish had created. What a buzz.

> **"I found a few bubblers in a tiny bay. Being the calm type, I legged it frantically back to the car to get a rod and some bait. I cast in and only had 10 minutes to wait before I got a bite."**

A short fight ensued before I had her safely in the net. She was a true English stunner and 34lb 8oz of very long, near-leather carp. I was delighted with the time she took to catch and the ease with which I caught her. I went back to my camp to fish all night with

This is the long, 34lb fish that I managed to stalk when the going was slow.

> My plan was to have a big baited area for two rods and be a bit more subtle with my third. I spodded a large area of hemp, crushed tiger nuts, Grubber pellets and various sizes of boilies. The mixture of sizes helps confuse the carp because they have to use different levels of effort for sucking up different-sized baits.

three rods and blanked. It just goes to show what you can achieve with a little effort. I've had a really good summer this year with many fine fish to over 40lb, both here and abroad.

French Fling

As well as the Berkshire pit, French fishing has really started to grip me over the last year or so.

The carp are definitely built to a larger scale over there and forties and fifties are in abundance. I had always been one of those very stubborn 'I only want to fish in England' carp anglers up until this point in my carp fishing career.

However, my brother-in-law had convinced me that we had to have a French fishing holiday, so that was that. After a bit of research we decided that our venue was going to be Forest Angling's Etang Des Royale.

The preparations were made and I was soon angling for the first time abroad. We took mainly air-dried Richworth Complex boilies with us and picked up hemp and pellet once we were out there.

I don't want to take up too much of my story with the French stuff, but it really was a trip to remember. From the off, I caught carp by night and day and in numbers too.

In total I managed to land 66 carp. The majority were over 20lb, with 20 over the 30lb mark, topped off with a stunning 42lb beast. The total weight was in excess of three-quarters of a ton - in one week. I was absolutely shattered; it was like a week of

39lb 2oz and the biggest of the five thirties hit.

A perfect-looking common from the Berkshire lake.

My most successful presentations have included stringers and my favourite Withy Pool rig.

endurance. This was my introduction to French carping, don't forget. That was it; I was hooked.

On my return, the editor of Total Carp, Marc Coulson, soon took the opportunity to show the pictures in his magazine. They were great and we had a really good response from the feature.

My next French trip was to Rootswood Sky Lake. I have since done a week session and a four-day session there. On both occasions I caught a mid-forty.

The four-day trip was in the middle of summer. Everything was green and the wildlife was abundant, and I made it my ambition to try and stalk a massive fifty-pounder.

I baited one area with 10mm boilies and a hemp/pellet combination. After leaving the area for two hours to settle, I returned to find fish feeding. I didn't stop to look what size they were, I just angled for them.

In no time at all I was latched into a fish of just under 30lb. Because of all the commotion there was not a fish left in the area, so I rebaited the spot and left it alone for another few hours. Would this tactic work, I wondered?

Gobsmacked

On my return I was completely gobsmacked. There was the biggest carp I had ever seen, four feet away from me and she was feeding hard. I was a trembling mess; she looked every ounce a 60lb fish. I waited and waited for a sensible opportunity to lower my rig onto the spot

nd then bingo, the coast was clear. That's it thought, the photo was already clear in my nind's eye.

I looked down the margin and there she vas, waddling back to my spot. I hid behind small tree, fully camouflaged with my 'ribal shreds on. If a normal person had een me I think they would have called the endarmerie (French police).

According to plan, the reel started hurning and I was latched onto this large ump. Wrong! There I was, trembling, and aying to myself over and over: "Please lon't come off, please don't come off!"

If you could have seen my face when a 5lb common surfaced you would have oared with laughter. There is an old saying: Don't count your chickens before they've atched." It simply hadn't occurred to me hat another fish might have picked up my ook bait! Oh well, next summer might be ny time for a 'sixty'!

Autumn's Arrival

Back to Berkshire, and the odd rumble of hunder and heavy showers signalled the rrival of autumn. Most wild animals know what's around the corner – the dreaded vinter.

Carp are no different and respond in a vay pleasing to most anglers, by feeding eavily. Being a consultant for Richworth, ve are usually given a new bait to test at he start of autumn. Last year saw the rrival of Ultraplex, Richworth's most cientific bait to date. We did not now how good this was going to

"The odd rumble of thunder signalled the arrivel of autumn. Most wild animals know what is around the corner – the dreaded winter. Carp are no different and respond similarly – by going on the feed!"

be. The field testers did their bit and they had a few. However, it was Ian Poole and myself that tested Ultraplex on our Berkshire lake. We have Ron Buss and Richworth to thank, because this was their brainchild. Basically, Ian and myself went at it full tilt.

Usually when testing a bait we use it in opposition to another for results. Just by picking up this bait I knew the carp would not be able to resist.

This was the start of my autumn campaign. Picture the scene, Pooley and myself are sat at the lake after casting out our wannabe bait. The head bailiff and two others turn up for a chat and immediately spot our new bait. In a typical childlike fashion they ask: "What's that?"

"Doh," I replied in Homer Simpson style. "This is the next revolution in carp fishing and you've seen it first."

"Mumble, mumble," came the muted reply.

"This is going to be the best big-fish boilie you will ever buy, " I said. With that they became more interested, literally stealing handfuls and sniffing, eating and carefully scrutinising them.

The next thing that happened was bang on time; my alarm burst into life as the two visitors to our swim looked on. Like a cocky ninja I jumped to it, feeling pretty happy with myself.

A big smirk soon turned to embarrassment, as I did not need to use my net for the 1lb roach that followed. Laughter, mickey taking and abuse followed and took some time to subside. Me and my big mouth!

That first autumn trip was not a disaster, though, because I slipped my net under 13 large carp. Among these were three 27s, two 28s, a 29 and three thirties to mid-thirty. I did chuckle about the roach though. Awesome!

"Welcome to Ultraplex," I thought one evening. This bait helped Pooley and me catch a huge amount of large carp in a total of 18 nights throughout that autumn. Combined, we managed 96 fish, with at least two-thirds of them being over the 24lb mark. The thirties list was also impressive, totalling 21.

My Sky Lake 'forty'. What a stunning-looking carp and one that I was very pleased with, for obvious reasons!

The Action Didn't Stop

As autumn matured, the action did not stop but inevitably it did ease slightly. We had basically caught half of the perceived stock in front of us by this time.

Usually at the start of November we have to work for our sponsors at the various carp shows and the like. I only fish weekends so hardly got my rods out until December. I have mixed thoughts about winter - I either hate it or really hate it!

I still enjoy going, don't get me wrong, but dark at 4pm, asleep by 7pm, awake by midnight, deliberating going for a pee for an hour because it's so cold, half an hour to get warm again and then it could rain for a full 12 hours - it's not much fun sometimes.

Like a real mate, Pooley decided to stay at home and catch up on his journalism. Yeah right! Like a real div, I made it my ambition to catch a winter mid-thirty, but I only managed one trip in December. My real campaign started on December 28th and what a session it turned out to be! It was minus 6°C and I caught nothing!

My next trip was the following weekend and milder weather was on the cards. I decided on the same swim that I had fished the previous weekend and all my lines were marked up ready to go. I opted for single bottom-bait Ultraplex boilies, to which I attached a small bag of mini Grubber pellets. Out they went, back to the spots. I spodded out a bit of hemp, crushed tigers and pellets and sat back to dream about the spring. Out of the blue, at midnight, my right-hand rod found itself attached to a large carp. A slow but powerful fight commenced and I eventually slipped the net under one of my real ambition fish - a 35lb-plus mirror carp called The Holiday Fish. She is called this because she was wrongly in the little lake on the site that is fished by the holiday anglers. She'd been moved there by a disgruntled angler who didn't join the syndicate. This was it, the last fish on my A-team list to catch. A mid-thirty in January - fantastic!

> **"This was it. A carp called the 'Holiday Fish'. She was the last one on my list and I'd caught her in January. After that I carried on fishing through February and endured some horrendous weather."**

Another Good Twenty

I had another good twenty that trip as well. I carried on my winter campaign, doing every weekend in February, and endured some horrendous weather throughout this period.

On one session the lake completely froze over, half an inch thick, before it snowed. Oh I love winter angling! At least there wasn't anyone else around and I had the lake to myself.

I did have some more success during February, though. A strong northeasterly wind was blowing on one session that cut you in half. Despite this, I opted to use a lot of pellet and hemp to try and get the fish moving.

That was my plan, and it worked. I had two takes; one was a common just short of mid-thirty and the other a 31lb mirror. I think that was the coldest I have ever been while playing a carp, but it was worth every painful moment.

Carp fishing does different things to different people. Me, I am completely nuts about it and probably always will be, no matter what time of year and whatever the weather. If I ever own a tackle shop I'll probably call it 'Four Seasons Angling'.

I hope you've enjoyed my story of a fishing year, it was a great one and I was lucky enough to catch lots of fish. Hopefully it will inspire you to get out there and do the same!

A mid-thirty taken in the winter – very nice!

Another thirty, stunning in its winter colours.

FOUR SEASONS IN ONE BAG!

Ultra-Plex is designed to stimulate fish feeding in all temperatures, even in the depths of Winter.
Our extensive tests have produced some unbelievable results, even when other popular baits and flavours have failed!

Made from totally natural powdered and liquid extracts with a unique blend of bird foods and fish meals. Ultra-plex is the best choice throughout the season if you want to keep catching consistently.

Ultra-Plex
- the ultimate all-year bait!

Available as: • Airo Pop-ups • Base mixes • Impact Boilie dips • Base Mix additives •Freezer baits • Shelf lifes and dumbells.

"During September and October last year, the bait produced no less than 21 UK thirties for Steve Renyard and myself, and it continued to catch fish right into the winter."
Ian Poole

IAN POOLE

STEVE RENYARD

For a free colour brochure containing all Richworth products, including our full range of Ultra-plex products, please send your name and address to;

Streamselect Ltd., Island farm Avenue, West Molesey, Surrey. KT8 2UZ

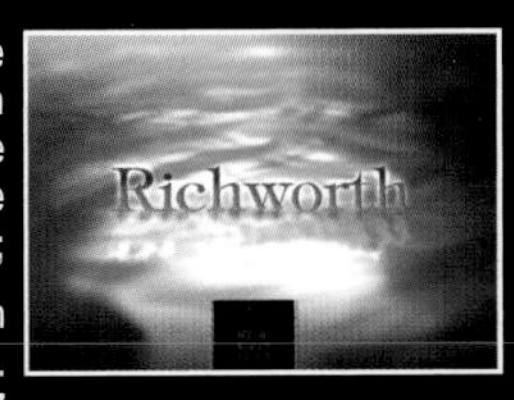

ULTRA-PLEX

Richworth DAYGLOW ULTRA-PLEX AIRO POP-UPS

Richworth WHO ELSE?

www.richworth.com

A scene that many of us can only dream of, as a group of 30lb carp take surface baits.

Big-Pit Tales

There are few pits more daunting than the 360-acre Sonning Eye. Dave Lane recounts an obsessive campaign chasing its most famous resident that took its name from the pit itself...

I've undertaken a lot of different campaign-style fishing over the years, the sort of fishing where I have targeted one particular fish, or water, and stayed there until I considered the job to well and truly done!

Some of the most exiting of these campaigns have been the ones like Wraysbury or Sonning, where I was aware of one or two big 'target fish' like Mary or The Eye but the bulk of the stock were still unknown to me.

The thrill of fishing under these conditions is indescribable. You know that the lake is capable of producing big fish and you live in eternal hope that the next run will produce an unknown monster. The stories of such monsters were obviously rife on Sonning, especially given that it was around 360 acres and therefore large enough to hold enough rumour, myth and legend to keep even a sceptic like me on tenterhooks for years.

When Sonning was launched onto the carp fishing scene with the publication of a picture of Andy Dodd holding a 52lb carp, caught in the spring of 2000, the rush for tickets took the local angling club by surprise and it was unclear whether or not we would get ours in time for the forthcoming season.

As it turned out, luck was on our side and Keith Jenkins and myself (along with most other anglers we knew) soon had our new permits and new dreams.

Reading Angling, which controlled the fishing at Sonning, only held permission for about a quarter of the bank space, the rest was gravel workings, sailing clubs or just plain out of bounds.

It soon became apparent, though, that there were people fishing these out-of-bounds areas. Whether or not they had permission remained to be seen but we made a mental note of it in case we needed the odd trip to the far side ourselves. Just to put it into perspective here, you could barely even see the far side of the lake and anglers fishing it were mere dots on the horizon – it took us weeks just to figure out how to get around there!

First Season

At the beginning of the first season, as we set up for the first time on our new home, all the fish were blatantly up at the shallow end of the lake and Keith and I could see them all bow waving about at range.

The shallow end was fished at a big disadvantage from the in-bounds section as the bar systems, that the fish could be seen using, were at extreme range. This meant that the level of accuracy needed to place a bait on top of a bar at well over 100 yards could not be attained from the bank. Boats were not allowed and we could see the fish but, unfortunately, not fish for them effectively. There was only one swim that covered the required ground and it sat out on a small peninsula at the end of the in-bounds section. Understandably, it was also very popular.

It also gave access to a small, snag-filled bay that would eventually prove a big draw to the carp, but that would not be until the following spring and at this time it was knowledge that we neither had nor needed.

The first big winds of the season came at the end of the second week and howled across a hundred acres of open water, sending massive white-capped waves crashing spectacularly into the sailing/ski-club bank. By standing on the ski-club jetty I managed to glimpse a couple of shapes moving deep down below the swell. The jetty bank was out of bounds to angling but I could fish the adjacent bank that also faced into the teeth of the gale. The swim I chose was in an area that was, technically, off limits but a quick chat with the guy who ran the ski club left me in no doubt that nobody particularly cared what I did as long as I kept my head down, which was fine by me.

Inland Sea

It was not so much a swim as a hole in the bushes and it absolutely screamed carp.

There was thick froth blowing up the bank where the waves had whipped the surface up and the water rocked with the effects of the big southwesterly wind pounding into this small corner of an inland sea! I simply flicked two baits out in front of me, both bottom baits and 20mm in size, one on the shelf and one at the bottom where it seemed to drop off into 10 feet or so of water. It was hard to ascertain anything in the conditions, so I threw a handful of bait around each one and hid myself by laying face down on the floor next to the rods and pulling a piece of camouflage netting over me and the rods. The thrill of that first run on a new water is indescribable, especially when you have no idea what may be on the end. Given the conditions and the fact that I could see the odd one cruise past in the turbulent margins, it was inevitable that it was going to happen.

Given the conditions and the fact that I could see the odd carp cruising past in the margins, it was inevitable that I'd catch one.

Nevertheless, I still nearly suffered a coronary when it did eventually rip off. I was laying on my belly with my head peering over the edge of the bank, straining for another glimpse of a fish in the coloured water, with the rod tips right next to my head, when one of them whipped around and line flew from the spool. The wind was so strong that it was all I could do to stand up against it, let alone play a very angry carp. The fish raged for a good 10 minutes before I managed to net him, fighting as if he had never felt a hook before and his very life depended on it. He really did put up an extraordinarily hard scrap and my knuckles were actually bleeding on my left hand as I tried to drag him into the margins for netting. The netting was the worst part of the lot. Actually pushing the net under the waves was a nightmare, as the wind kept throwing it back up in the air and into the branches above me. The wind was so strong that clouds of spray were being thrown up from the margins and soaking me in the process. Somehow I managed to get him into the net and up onto the bank. My first fish from a new water and it was an immaculate, and new personal best, common of 33lb 8oz! A few hours later I took another common of 25lb from the same spot and I even managed to follow this up with a scraper twenty the next morning! It was a massive feeling of relief to know that I had a rig and a bait that

Now you see me... not!

would, and could, do the business. All that remained to do was find a few more spots that might produce. After all, I could hardly rely on a gale-force southwesterly every week of the season could I?

In the past I have been very mobile in my approach to big pits, always putting myself where I thought the fish were at any given time. At first, bolstered by my recent results with the commons, I thought this would also be the method on Sonning. As it turned out, this was definitely not the case and it became obvious that I would need to adopt a different outlook altogether.

There is so much water that is either out of bounds, or merely out of range, that mobility would only work when the fish were actually accessible. Vast areas were untouchable and location alone would not be enough to secure results. Only one or two wind directions would bring the fish within range of the in-bounds bank and most of the visible bars and features were too far out. I figured that if I could persuade them to stay in, or at least revisit, an area on a fairly regular basis then I would stand a better chance.

It took a while to find the ideal spot to bait and when it did materialise it was the fish that picked the area rather than us.

During a night session in a new area and on a fresh wind, Keith managed to catch his first fish from the water and lost another one so we decided that this would be as good an area as any to bait up. It was an area that was not usually fished. In fact, Keith had to cut out a swim to reach the water's edge and the next week we made another one a few yards further along to the left. We intended to create a feeding area of our own, by the introduction of masses of bait, to see if we could persuade the fish to keep returning to the area, even in the wrong weather conditions.

Five Bar Trick

The area was subsequently plumbed to death over the next few weeks and we discovered a system of five bars that, after weaving their way from miles away, all ended up a mere 30 yards out, in front of our two new swims.

The various humps and bumps at their ends were heavily weeded all around but perfectly fishable on the tops. At first, they had appeared as one bar running across in front of us but careful plumbing had provided us with the knowledge that would lead us to a string of captures and the perfect area for our campaign.

Although Keith and I are both lovers of 'a bit of bait', I don't think we had ever baited like that before, or since, as we realised very quickly that the only way to make a real difference was going to be using 'lots' of bait. Massive bream were also present in numbers and no amount of bait appeared to deter them. Vast quantities of 20mm Assassin-8 was deposited onto the bars and subsequently eaten by something or another every night. It was not unusual to put out 10kg per angler, per night!

The fish were obviously using the bars as roads and making their way down the lake under the cover of darkness. The strange thing was, they would only use one or two of the roads per night, and never come at all in

Travelling light was often the name of the game.

Off the mark... and in some style.

My first recapture, but still a stunning fish.

I'd found The Eye, and it looked massive.

the daytime. I picked off the odd one in the morning to start with but pretty soon the bite time shrank to a period between 11pm and about 3am. It was obvious that the fish were spending the daytimes in a totally different area and only venturing along the bars for a feed-up at night. It got so predictable in the end that I changed my entire sessions to coincide with the feeding spells.

Bream Bother

I managed to clock up an incredible 19 carp from Sonning that first year. Some nights I would have six bream on the trot and then a carp about midnight, bait up again in the dark, then suffer another couple of bream before bagging another carp in the early hours.

Most of the fish were ex river fish that had found their way in from the Thames, which ran right alongside one bank of Sonning. These were mainly low twenties but very pretty fish all the same.

We knew that the big old 50-pounder would turn up eventually; a fish of that size would not ignore baiting like that for very long. I just hoped that it wasn't one of the fish we had already lost!

Due to the heavy weed we had dropped a few, not too many, but one that I had lost I felt convinced was a very big fish. Eventually, as we had predicted, the big fella waddled his way along the bar system and into my swim for a big munch-up but fate was to deal me a bad card that night and deny me the result that I had so patiently waited for.

I had arrived, as usual, on the Thursday morning, only to find that one of the other regulars had taken time off work, specifically to get to my swim a day before me and try his luck on the area that was, by now, stripped bald by the constant baiting and feeding activity. Obviously our captures were not going unnoticed and our area was very much in demand. Conditions were perfect on this particular weekend, with a big northerly wind forecast for the second night of my session. Sure enough, by first light, on the day after the wind, it was all over and 52lb of mirror carp, its sides bright red from all of my Assassin-8 boilies it had been eating, was laying on the bank in my swim. Unfortunately, I was on the wrong side of the camera!

I was very upset at having to watch somebody else reap the rewards for all of our hard work but that's the way it goes sometimes!

After winter had passed and the flooding that plagued the county had eventually subsided, we set back out for Sonning and another campaign for The Eye was underway.

Obviously we were dubious about fishing the same areas as last year, as they were now well known and would be under constant pressure from other anglers, so we set out to try and find the fish in another area altogether.

We had no experience of spring on Sonning at all and it was, once again, all very fresh and exciting.

> **"After winter had passed and the floods that plagued the county had subsided, we headed back to Sonning."**

The mobile approach seemed to be the best option to start with as fish in big pits tend to move around a lot at this time of year, especially before the spawning urges set in. Unlike later in the year, when the food supplies can persuade fish to stay in certain sections of the pit, different areas come in to play and a new wind can literally move fish for miles!

By the end of April the fish started to appear regularly, warming their bodies in the strengthening sunlight.

Spawning Time

Anglers were picking off the odd one here and there, particularly on the shallows in a massive bay that sits at the head of the pit.

As is often the way in spring, the fish had noticeably split into two size groups for spawning. Although spawning was still some way off, the fish start to congregate with others of their own stamp to feed, laze, and generally prepare for the glorious, once-a-year orgy that inevitably follows.

On Sonning the fish had been merrily doing there own thing for years, with only a handful of anglers to disturb them, so I was

Baiting the edge of the vast pit.

gambling that they were well set in their ways. It was obvious that only the small ones were left on the shallows and I assumed that this was the area they had chosen for spawning. The bigger fish had to be all together somewhere else and the only way to find out where was to go exploring.

There were certainly plenty of areas to explore and I walked for miles, looking for that inevitable 'safe area' where the biggest and strongest would be preparing themselves for a big feed-up and then sex!

It came as no surprise really that when I did eventually find them they were tucked up safely in the out-of-bounds area. It was the ideal spot really; snaggy, sheltered, and facing the sun. It was set apart from the workings area by a new, interconnected pit of about eight acres. This had the effect of isolating the snaggy bay out on a peninsula where hardly anybody went.

Jungle Warfare

Keeping low, to avoid attracting any unwanted attention, I battled my way through some heavy undergrowth and came out directly behind a large section of the snags and, as I poked my head through the first gap in the bushes, I saw him.

He was just laying there, five feet below me, just under the surface, in crystal-clear water. I had never, ever, seen anything so impressive in my life!

I'd never seen a carp so wide before, for the pure reason that there isn't another carp that wide in the entire country. It was immense, monstrous, almost ridiculous, and for some reason very scary!

Further along in the snags I could see other good fish as well, and after a quick and very shaky reconnaissance crawl, I knew I'd found THE area where they would sun themselves and warm up prior to spawning in a few weeks' time.

There was no way on earth that they were ever going to feed actually in the snags. Even if they did, landing them would be a nightmare.

A network of bars made their way into this snaggy area and it was obviously that I'd pick the fish off as they came in and left every morning and evening, at least that was the plan! I was so close to the actual fish that I had to conceal all my tackle by camouflaging every single item I possessed. This also helped with the small matter of whether I was actually supposed to be in this area in the first place!

I saw no point in baiting heavily. The fish were already here and I was assuming that they would come here every day until the spawning ritual, which would take place as soon as the water temperatures stabilised at a level that they found ideal to drop their load, probably out among the weed beds at the back of this large bay. I knew that my mate CP was heavily baiting an area in the next section along, about 600 yards away by water and the other side of a chain of islands. I decided to fish by another method entirely and use attractor-bait pop-ups placed on the highest points of the various bars and hope to ambush the carp in transit. I was after a quick result and thought that this would offer me the best chance.

That first session when I discovered the fish, about 20 carp in all, I only had one night remaining and I set up in a swim about 60 yards away from the snags and waited as the evening fell and they slowly moved off. To my absolute horror the fish took an entirely different route out of the bay to what I had anticipated, following the bars in the opposite direction and missing my carefully laid traps by about 300 yards!

A Sonning brace.

> **"He was just laying there, five feet below me, just under the surface. I had never, ever, seen anything quite so impressive in my life!"**

Bow Waves

Luckily, the morning route was a bit more favourable and, at about 4am, I spotted the first carp, bow waving into the bay about 200 yards behind my baits, blatantly following the transit routes and heading for my left-hand bait. Half an hour, and three or four bow waves later, the left-hand rod burst into life as a 24lb mirror fell for a Fruit-Tella pop-up. Within an hour the rest of the fish had made it to the sanctuary of the snags and I could only spend the day watching and photographing them in their haven before setting off home. I was quite unlucky really with the size of my fish, as I don't reckon there was much below that weight left in the group, but I certainly wasn't complaining. I just prayed that they would still be there

I know you're out there... somewhere.

It was daunting to say the least.

> **I gave up and walked round to CP's swim. He was yelling and punching the air – I knew he'd caught The Eye.**

when I returned in five days' time.

As luck would have it, I returned to find the scene exactly as I had left it. I'd told nobody of my capture and the fish were still there, unmolested and lazing in the sun. That session was a disaster. I lost two fish the first morning and one on the second, before landing a 27lb mirror that I had caught the previous year from the old swim. This, incredibly, was my first and only repeat capture from Sonning but was, probably, one of the nicest-looking fish I've ever caught, so I didn't mind too much.

The lost fish irked me no end. They were all lost due to the gravel bars in one way or another; my only consolation was that the big fella was still in the snags and obviously not one of the ones that I'd lost. It was an incredible sight to be so close to such a colossal carp. I couldn't even guess at the weight he may be, all I knew was that he was far bigger than anything I'd ever seen before. What a way to spend a day though, laying on my belly staring eyeball to eyeball with a big, 50lb fish. It was a good opportunity to see what other beasts the lake held as well, although I was surprised to see how few other large fish there were. The second biggest was the known forty that had been captured and just over 40lb the previous year. The next one was another fish that didn't look far short of the 40lb mark, although she was obviously holding a fair amount of spawn; it had a distinctive large plate scale near the vent that I knew I'd recognise on the bank. From these fish down it was really only a couple of mid-thirty mirrors and two or three good commons, two of which I had already had at 33lb and 31lb. It seemed that the big one was a breed on its own and was obviously a completely different strain to any of the other fish there. He was also in a completely different size bracket and really did dwarf everything else he swam past.

That evening they made their way out of the bay along their normal routes. The big 'un was the last to leave and was really getting obscenely large now. Surely it couldn't be long before they started to spawn, the weather was very settled and constantly warm and sunny. That night I went and spent some time in CP's swim. I hadn't even told him about all the action I'd received that session, I was a bit pissed off about losing so many fish and I wanted a chance at the big 'un before shouting too loud about the takes I was receiving. I suppose it was a case of once bitten twice shy after the previous year's fiasco. Chris had only had one small common so far this year, despite using massive quantities of bait.

The next morning I was sitting up and waiting at first light for the fish to appear as usual but they didn't show. By eight o'clock I knew something was wrong. Just then CP ran into the swim all excited, saying he'd just had a 37-pounder and lost a big common at the net. I told him I'd be around in an hour when I was sure that my chances of a take were not coming.

Pet Dog

After half an hour, and with no sightings, I gave up and walked around to his swim, passing him in the field. He was over the other side, running around yelling and punching the air – I knew! What I couldn't have known was the weight. That fish that I had had in my swim like a pet dog for two weeks turned out to be the second-largest carp in the land and weighed in at a colossal 57lb! What a morning for CP, all that hard work had paid off in the end and I had learnt a valuable lesson. Unfortunately, it was one that I already knew but had ignored. The big fish always come to the big, prebaited areas. Time and time again it happens and CP had certainly put some bait in his swim over the last few weeks and that had obviously been where they went every night. It had just been this final morning before spawning that they threw caution to the wind and ate everything in sight. A 57lb mirror a 37lb mirror and a big common lost at the net, an excellent result for Chris. He had played it right, done the hard work and had his just rewards. My turn would surely come, wouldn't it? I started my own baiting campaign that very afternoon. I picked a spot near to the gap where the fish had had to pass to get from my bay into Chris's and found the perfect feature in the form of a double hump at about 60-yards range. It was in the middle of the 'route' and the fish could hardly fail to notice it as they

I coud see the carp approaching my bait.

I tried everything I could to blend in.

A stunning, first-year common.

moved to and fro up the pit. I didn't muck about with the bait either, piling in as much as I could carry and, over a four-week period, I must have put in 150kg of boilies and pellets. This may seem an awful lot of bait, especially as I was only catching bream, but I could tell that every week the spot would have changed dramatically. The silt and clay that held the stones that formed the hump together was being eroded by the constant attentions of fish. What started out as a clay hump with gravel mixed in, ended up as a pile of bricks and rubble. In fact, if I had continued, I think it may have collapsed! During my weeks fishing the little swim that I had cut out for myself, I picked off about eight carp by fishing pop-ups at range up against the stringy weed. In fact, it was only when this weed started to die off that I saw visible signs of carp at night over the hump.

No Poaching!

The swim itself was totally hidden away and could not be seen from anywhere. I was not being 'poached' again this year! All my gear was still camouflaged from the old swim and I trained the weeds to grow over an old bivvy that I left up in the swim, so I blended in nicely. All of the fish I had picked off from the bars at range had been small ones but I was determined that eventually the bait would draw the big fella in and this time I was not going to miss out. Wherever the fish went in this section of the lake they would have to pass through this gap to change areas or to utilise the main section of water. There were only two ways in and out and from my observations I knew that this route was used frequently. Occasionally, I arrive earlier if I can and this particular week I arrived at 3am on the Wednesday. I wanted to put out a lot of bait and fish over the top of it for a few days to see what was visiting the hump. Often, I would bait heaviest when I left but this week I intended to really go for it and put out 25kg of bait on the hump.

"It was the dead of night when nothing dares make a sound. Nothing that is apart from a big old carp that I was attempting to net."

Mosquito Nightmare

The mosquitoes were a nightmare due to the overgrown nature of the swim and their absolute love of my blood! By about midnight, total sleep depravation and near malaria from a thousand mosquito bites was beginning to take its toll and I staggered back to my swim for some much-needed kip. It felt as if I had only been asleep for a few minutes when a squawking alarm sent me hurtling into the makeshift mosquito netting hanging from my bivvy and depositing me, thrashing, onto the floor trying to free myself. Eventually I broke free and struck into my first run from the hump. I must have actually been asleep for longer than I thought, as the total silence all around told me it was that dead time of night, around 3am, when nothing seems to dare make a sound. Nothing that is apart from a big old carp that was making a sound like a drowning pig as I attempted to drag him into the net. The fight had just been a display of kiting and plodding that, had I been more awake, would have told me it was a big fish. It was only when I stuck my hand in the net and felt a bloody great pop-eye that I realised for sure that I'd got him. A total of 350 acres of water, 12 months of hard work and a lorry load of bait and finally I'd got him! Keith arrived in the swim minutes later having been awoken by my sounder box that I'd accidentally left in his swim the night before. He found me laying across a mountain of beached whale, shouting: "I've bloody got him!" over and over again, until I was finally convinced that I had!

By the time we had sacked him safely and phoned everyone silly enough to answer at that time of the morning, it was getting light enough to do the rituals of weighing and photographing. I couldn't even lift him off the ground, so Keith hoisted him up and the needle span around to 55lb, which made him a new personal-best 'whale' as well as the culmination of the most intense and bizarre campaign that I think I've ever undertaken. Once again the big, baited spot produced the big 'un but this time it was the only fish to come from it!

It made me wonder how many times he'd visited the area before and how he had managed to 'get away with it' so many times. However, they were thoughts for another day, that day was for celebrating!

The Eye, and a new PB at 55lb. I was elated and decided that it was time to celebrate!

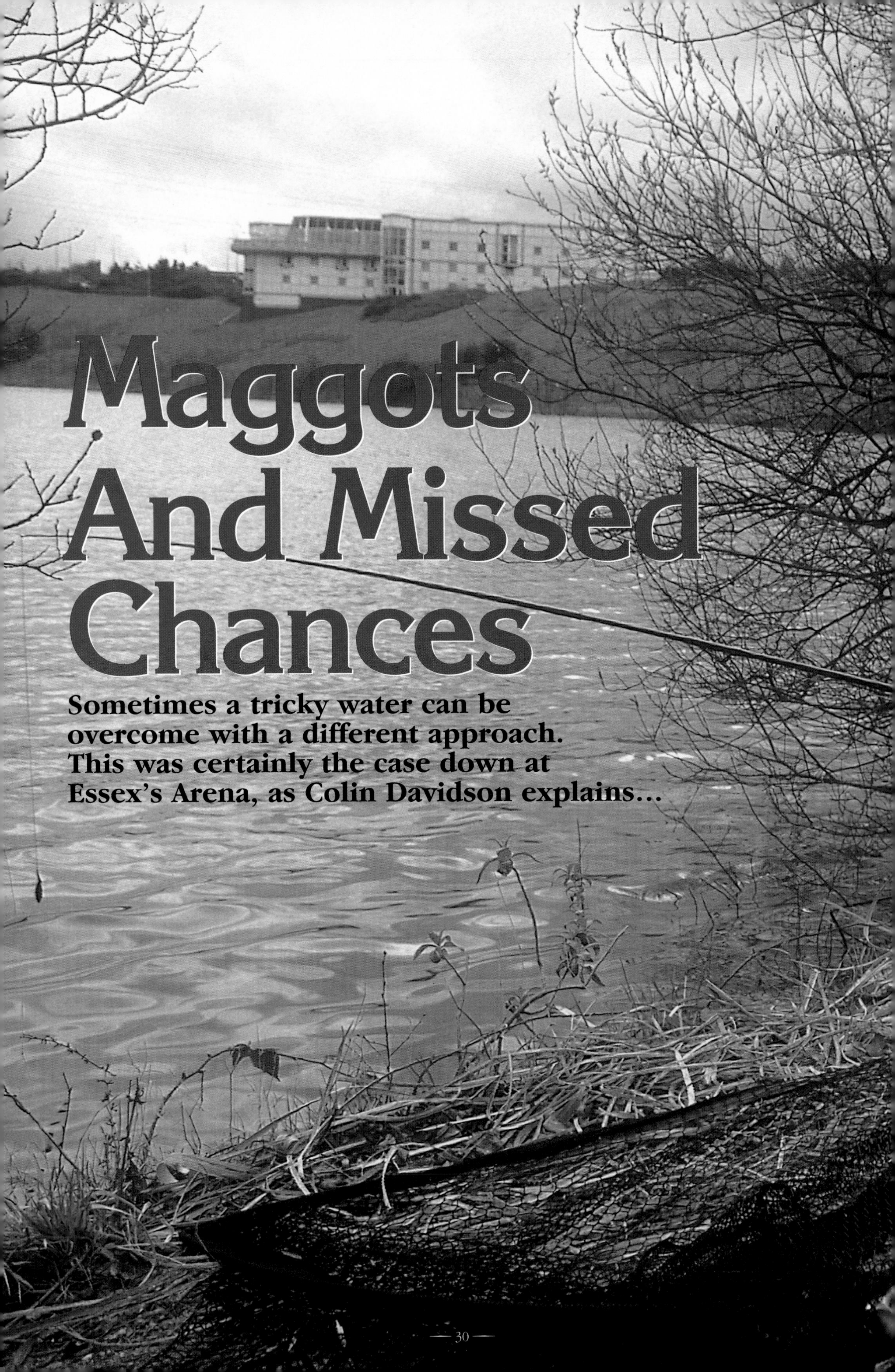

Maggots And Missed Chances

Sometimes a tricky water can be overcome with a different approach. This was certainly the case down at Essex's Arena, as Colin Davidson explains…

Tucked behind the end of the car park of Thurrock Services, next to the M25, the Essex Arena was never going to stand out for its beauty. It was more Bosnia by day and Benidorm by night.

On one bank you spent your time looking at a permanently illuminated hotel at the top of a steep hill, behind you it would be roaring stock-car engines, thumping music and cheering crowds from the Arena racetrack. Surrounded by cliffs covered in scrub, dirt tracks and waste ground, you didn't join for the scenery.

My ticket came through in 2000 thanks to my old mate Phil, a bailiff at the time. The fish were coming on and it seemed to have become an absolute thirties factory and full of big commons. Growth rates weren't unconnected to the crayfish explosion. Infested with turks rather than the more-common signal reds, the carp were thriving.

I'd heard horror stories about the crays and had never fished a water with the pesky lobsters in before. I'd been told half an hour was all you got from the hardest bait you could make, tigers and peanuts got eaten the same. There was no defence against them and the entire lake bed was supposed to be virtually crawling. It sounded more science fiction than fishing.

Crayfish Problems

On my first trip I didn't know what to expect and set up on the south bank, the shallowest end of the 15 acres. Out went the baits for the afternoon and nosing around in the deep, clear margins in front of the swim I spied a crayfish sitting on the bottom. I lobbed a tutti in and it fluttered down to rest a foot away from him. I figured he would be a good indicator as to how quickly my hook baits were being whittled down. Four hours later he'd shown no interest, which surprised me. It was only when I wound in all my rigs with nothing on the hairs that I finally twigged he was dead. He'd probably been disentangled from a rig by the last angler in the swim, tossed back in and had just happened to land upright!

I caught a carp on my first night trip, an 18-pounder, but getting your head around sitting behind buzzers was difficult when you knew what was happening to your hook bait. I was using Fox Microns at the time and every time a hook bait went out it only took a couple of minutes before you saw that telltale flashing LED from a tiny drop back that told you a lobster was pulling your hooklength. It was a truly horrendous crayfish problem.

The road 'pool' after the spring flooding.

Arena had a four-day and four-night maximum stay at the time, and it was a keenly fought battleground for the local bait wars. There were more free and cheap bags of boilies and pellets doing the rounds than any other lake I've fished since. Each team had a few full-timers who would normally be found in one of the favoured swims, like the Point or Bailiff's, with bucket after bucket of bait.

I didn't have that sort of time, wasn't any good at spodding and, from what I could see, I didn't think big baited areas were working very well. It was the clarity of the water on Arena that really helped me sort them out. Being a chalk pit, it was like tap water almost all of the year, and with so many snaggy, inaccessible areas, with deep, clear margins, you could always find fish drifting along the edges. With so much bivvying up and spodding going on there were substantial parts of the lake that weren't really being fished. The north bank was almost completely ignored, yet everywhere I sat for half an hour and kept my eyes open I'd see a few carp. I'd never fished any venues that allowed you to see the carp so closely and so clearly.

Feeding Carp

On one of my early visits I walked past a bloke plotted up on the Point who was obviously filling it in. Carrying on down the bank, I watched a few carp drifting in and out of the margins. It wasn't a swim as such and involved climbing down plenty of brambles and a pretty hairy slope to get down to the water. I watched them for a while, climbed back up the bank and went and got a rod, mat, net and bait bucket and negotiated all the brambles a third time to get a bait in position. There were snags either side that I could see but a large open shelf and sunken swim platform in the middle – plenty of room to play a carp in.

A pouchful of Frenzied Hemp and a pouchful of frozen red maggots went in, plus a few chopped Mainline Grange boilies. The carp came back in within minutes and started hoovering the bait up. I was perched awkwardly on some brambles a few feet above the water with my heart thumping, certain I was going to catch one. After a couple of minutes I watched a 20-pounder approach the hook bait and then turn away. It didn't spook; it just didn't eat it. I'd rigged up with my hard boilie hook baits and wrapped them in paste, which I was very confident in, but after another couple of refusals from different fish it was clear these carp weren't overexcited about my offering.

After another 10 minutes of them feeding hard and not getting caught, I wound the rig out, took the boilies off and threaded a load of maggots up the hair instead. It was a bit of a botch job and looked like Marge Simpson's hair. When the coast was clear I lowered the hook bait in and fed more hemp and maggots. Just as I turned to slacken the line and try and find some brambles to wedge the rod into, I spied a common come drifting back in over the bait just a few yards away from me. I froze, convinced he was going to spook. Instead he made a beeline for the hook bait and snaffled it.

We fought for a few minutes but after the lead dropped off the clip and I'd disentangled

It's a thrill watching fish like this pick up your hook bait.

The Weekend fish.

First trip and a common on the maggots.

the net from the brambles it was game over. I was so excited to have seen him take the hook bait at such close quarters. The way that fish had homed in on the bunch of maggots was incredible.

The more I thought about it, the more logical it was. Arena carp had probably rarely seen maggots, other than from the odd perch and roach angler. No right-minded carp angler would cast maggots out into a deep pit full of crayfish - you'd need your head tested. But in the edge you could see what was going on, so you'd know you'd always got a hook bait on. It was so simple it was perfect - fish for them where you could see the carp and the crays and you could fish with anything. Plus, there seemed little doubt that Arena carp were a lot more excitable with maggots than they were with boilies.

Head Scratching

I carried my carp back to the Point and weighed it. There was a little flurry of activity to the rods fished out into the lake, with three scraper 20lb commons in quick succession from a big spodded area. The angler concerned was understandably well chuffed and made the comment that Arena carp had always liked a big bed of bait and that was the way to catch them. I walked away scratching my head. I'd fished for 20 minutes and caught one, admittedly a bit smaller. This bloke had camped for three days and nights, and spodded for four or five hours a day, and they were his first bites. It didn't strike me as the best way to do it. I went away dead set on coming back with more maggots and fishing in the edge.

Next time down I was straight on to the overgrown north bank. Instead of taking three rods and all the usual session gear I took one rod, a net, a sling-style unhooking mat and chucked a drink, scales and camera inside it. I baited a few spots and sat down to watch and wait. The action started soonest in a little gap called the Pampas Grass swim, which turned out to be one of the most reliable spots for getting something feeding, although perversely a poor spot for bigger fish. The carp were demolishing the hemp and maggots I'd put in. I chucked a few

This claw shows the size of the crays!

maggots over the top of them and, as they drifted off, lowered a rig in, slackened everything off and waited for the carp to come back.

It didn't take long and half a dozen carp came in and started grazing again. The biggest of them, a pale, barrel-shaped common twisted and turned awkwardly as it hooked itself and suddenly the spool was spinning. At 25lb it was a great feeling to see the whole thing go to plan from start to finish.

Watching carp feeding over a hook bait in the edge of a clear pit is still the ultimate excitement to me, but back then it was something completely new. I'd been brought up fishing on the coloured waters of the northwest, and the big carp waters I'd fished since moving south didn't allow visual fishing like Arena. The whole thing was fascinating; recognising the different fish, trying to guess which was the biggest, seeing if there were any spots in the swim that a bigger fish frequented that might give me a better chance of hooking him.

Frenzied Hemp

I loved every minute of it and spent most of that summer walking around with an unhooking mat over my shoulder, with one rod, feeding hemp and maggots and then farming the spots through the day. I'm thin at the best of times but, added to the constant laps around the lake, which probably amounted to a mile or two, I got so caught up in the fishing I kept forgetting to eat, I was half a stone lighter.

It took a few laps to work out some of the better spots, but there were so many clean gravel shelves between snaggy bushes that I was pretty spoilt for choice. I quickly got into a routine of feeding lots of spots at the start of the day and then checking for carp with their tails in the air. The Frenzied Hemp was brilliant, it held their attention for so long that one handful in each spot would get them ripping the bottom up and keeping on coming back to look for more.

Each area of the lake had its moments and all the swims had their own peculiarities. The Pampas Grass was always productive, but mostly smaller fish, and I only ever had one 30-pounder feeding in there. Nevertheless, it was a good indicator swim. You could always tell it was going to be a difficult day when nothing came in to the Pampas Grass and after an hour or two you would be watching advancing crayfish and sometimes just make out a tench and perch that seemed to live nearby. Both were pretty big, the tench always hanging back in the deeper water and only taking very occasional maggots from the far edge of the baited area. The perch was a pretty handsome fellow but I've no idea how big he was. He picked my hook bait up once and I pulled the line and shook him off in case

"The Frenzied Hemp was brilliant and held their attention for so long that one handful would have them ripping up the bottom."

there were any carp about. I still regret that, I've not had a 3lb perch to this day!

Carp Corners

I worked it out as I went along, quickly adopting two pairs of polarising glasses; dark lenses for the day and the bright yellow Fox lenses for low light, so I could still see in the evenings or the first few hours of the day. The rod was swapped to a Daiwa Interline, which, rather than having rings, had the main line running through it. This meant that I didn't need to worry about the line getting caught in branches or bankside foliage when positioning rigs or lying the rod on the floor.

What was interesting was the Arena carp's obvious love of corners. Most of the original swims had been flooded by rising water levels. Fresh swims were built, leaving old ones underwater in front of them. They were perfect carp-feeding tables, especially given that they often had submerged bushes or reeds growing around them. Some days the carp would come and take you on over the sunken swims. There would often be a small groove running along the boarded outers of these sunken swims and I'd try and get the lead and line to sit down in it to make it less obvious. Other days they seemed to stay deeper, in front of the swims themselves. These would be more difficult days because you couldn't see the hook bait and crayfish would occasionally sneak in and strip the hair. You'd know you had a problem when the line tightened and dropped slack, then tightened again, as a cray tried to pull the food back to his hole or the safety of the underwater planks.

"Most of the original swims had been flooded and were left there when new ones were built. These were perfect carp-feeding tables."

It wasn't all non-stop action and it was as memorable a time for some of the carp I missed out on. I saw a lot of good carp in the edges on Arena but one that was noticeable by his absence was Nelson, the big fella. He was 45lb and very distinctive, with a crooked back, but not once did I see him in the margin over any of my spots. Some of the other big boys and girls were keener and, I'm sorry to say, tucked me up like a good 'un on more than one occasion.

Because the maggots-in-the-edge thing came about through opportunism, I kept on with exactly the same end tackle I'd used from the very first fish. With hindsight, I cringe at how inappropriate it was. I was (and still am) a big fan of running leads, and I was just running a 3oz lead straight along to a shock bead on the end of a 3ft Big Fish Adventure leadcore leader. With six inches of 10lb Pro Gold and a knotless knot to a Raptor T6, it was job done. Slack lines with a running lead when you're encouraging fish to hoover over small food items is as far from ideal as you could get. However, because I was catching fish and had seen it work so well, so many times, I didn't stop and question the efficiency of the rig. Nowadays I'd be more likely to have a 5oz drop-off inline and a 3in hooklength to really make their eyes water. Back then it was all such a new game that I missed such a fundamental trick and, as a result, missed out on some very special fish.

Hit List

The fish I really wanted was called QT, a mirror of around 38lb to 40lb, deep sided and exactly the same shape as Yateley's Bazil. It was an absolute gem of a carp and I came so close to him on a couple of occasions that it pains me to think about it even now. He made a charlie of me in front of the Dugout and again in the Daisies. It just hadn't occurred to me how inefficient my hooking arrangement was. When I twigged that there were occasions I was being repeatedly picked up and ejected with ease, I'd tried upping the baiting levels to encourage them to feed harder and bring about the mistake. Unfortunately, by putting more hemp in I was probably making the situation even worse.

It was on Arena that I saw first hand the differences in the way carp feed. Just enough hemp to fill the palm of your hand was more than enough, any more and they seemed to get into the hypnotic hoovering routine.

The big common, Four Eyes, was another near miss, and when a common is anywhere between 39lb and 40lb, and you see them doing you up, you don't forget it very quickly. I'd been wandering for a few hours early evening and hadn't seen much coming over my spots. I dumped my gear under the single big tree on the Point and stopped for a drink and a sit down. After a few minutes I saw a small group of carp swim just along

Nelson – I never found this fish in the edge.

The Royal Box swim, with its views of the Arena.

Another common at 28lb and caught on boilies.

he front of the submerged swim in front of he swim. Bearing in mind the Point had the car park behind it, and virtually zero cover, I vas a bit surprised. I fed a handful of hemp on the sunken swim and crept back under he tree, where I was partially hidden.

Sunken Swim

A few minutes later they came back, and here was an obvious reaction to the bait, even though they didn't hang around. A few minutes more, and a few more flypasts, and he first fish, a common around 22lb, came over the sunken-swim area. Several times he swam slowly around the perimeter of the boards, and I was sure he was looking for tackle or line. Eventually he settled and they all began to feed, including what was obviously Four Eyes – she was huge. It was the first time I'd seen her close up, and to this day she is the most perfect common I've seen. My problem was I had no maggots with me. There was no way I could get home and back to get some from the freezer because as soon as anyone drove into the car park the chance would be gone. All I could think to do was mix some Solar Bag Mix with water to make a paste to wrap around a boilie and hopefully make it more attractive.

It just wasn't good enough and seeing that common with its tail lobe poking out of the water, six feet from the bank, in front of one of the most popular swims, was soul destroying. I must have been picked up repeatedly but that common didn't flinch. After they drifted away I repositioned the bait. Several of the fish were perversely swimming up the flooded steps to get on to the swim platform, so I laid the rig in the groove behind the board of the top step and balanced the hook bait on the top step's lip. The first carp back in swam straight up the steps according to plan, picked it up, spat it in an instant, bolted and took all the others with it! Sometimes it just isn't meant to be…

However, there were plenty of good days too. On one trip I had so many fish going in so many places, I helped myself to eight carp from seven different swims by mid-afternoon, with four twenties, the best being the Weekend Fish at 28lb – all on the magic red wrigglers.

The Oak Fish at 34lb 12oz – stunning.

"As Neil arrived in my swim my rod went skidding across the floor from another 20lb common tearing off with my bait."

It was a Friday and I was off to the Exiles Fish-in at West Stow in Suffolk and Neil Waite was meeting me at Arena. As he arrived, my rod went skidding along the floor from another 20lb common stalked on the concrete slipway by the Bailiffs swim behind my car. In the next hour I added another couple of twenties from the Bailiff's, behind buzzers on boilies, including another 28-pounder, a common. It was one of those barmy trips where everything was going so well I couldn't put a foot wrong. My mate Phil had been on the phone asking how I was getting on, and when another member asked him where I was catching them all from, Phil explained it would be easier to tell him which swims I wasn't catching them in… I was working hard for my fish but that comment still makes me smile.

All Change

The following year it was all change at Arena, and with the water level having risen by six feet there was a serious amount of cold water that would take some warming in the spring. The lake had even sprung a leak and formed a pool about a hundred yards long, flooded over the roadway that led to the Point swim and car park. The carp were quick

GATES TO BE LOCKED AT ALL TIMES
ARENA SYNDICATE KEEP OUT
LAKE CLOSED UNTIL FURTHER NOTICE

Nuff said...

Fish like this will be sorely missed.

to come in and investigate, with several of the early fish being caught on what was effectively the car park – Arena was a bizarre venue in every way.

I fished a bit behind rods, and managed the first 30-pounder of the season with the Silver Common at 33lb, and the stunning Oak Fish at 34lb plus on maize off the flooded road. All the while I was checking around the edges looking for chances to mug them close in on maggots again, and eventually I started to see fish with more regularity.

I turned up for my usual Tuesday day trip and did the now-familiar lap of the lake and primed all the spots that had produced well the year before. Several hours later all that had shown any interest were crayfish. In front of the flooded-road pool, but in the main lake, I saw very occasional carp swimming up and down, following the line of the submerged bushes that were on dry land the season before. I baited with the usual handful of maggots and hemp and stood behind a solitary tree.

A personal-best common that I will be a little sad to ever beat.

Sniffing Around

It was frustrating in the extreme, and as the sun got higher in the sky it was clear that the carp were in a very difficult mood. After a couple of hours the only carp I'd seen had been big doubles and the odd low twenty. All of them looked to me like males that were intent on sniffing around after females – there was a purpose to their swimming that suggested their minds were elsewhere.

"She was huge, although I had never seen her on the bank before. Even Grant, who was an Arena veteran, said how big she looked."

Eventually, one dark mirror stopped and had a very brief root around over the spot. Then, as quickly as he'd dipped down, he was off again. It was infuriating and after another couple of very brief moments of the same carp nosing around for a mouthful in the following hour, I began to get quite wound up by him.

He was the only carp I'd seen that day that was even prepared to look at food. The next few times he drifted past I watched him very carefully. When he had gone I moved the hook bait a few feet to a small area that he'd nosed around a couple of times. Back behind the tree and we were back to the waiting game, at which point this troublesome carp then had a good couple of mouthfuls from exactly where the rig had been moved from. By this time it was becoming a personal contest and I was swearing under my breath.

New platforms were built where the old ones flooded.

By early afternoon I was really running out of patience, but still determined to catch the one carp that looked like he might take a hook bait. Unexpectedly, a substantial shape drifted into the swim from the left-hand side, right underneath me. It was twice the size of any of the carp I'd seen so far, and by the length and shape of it, a common – it had to be the Essy Common. It was so close I didn't dare move a muscle. She drifted straight in to the shallow, clear water and started grubbing around, picking up the maggots and hemp that had been all but ignored all day.

She was so close that as she hoovered along the bottom I saw her lips go, in what seemed like slow motion, over my bunch of maggots, them disappear into her mouth, then she righted herself, and the semi-fixed lead lifted off the bottom underneath her. For a split second nothing happened, and I couldn't believe what I was seeing as the lead hung on the short hooklength directly under her. Suddenly we were in real time again and the rod went skidding along the floor as a she turned, kicked her tail once, and bolted out of the margins. I grabbed the rod and immediately clamped on the spool to stop her taking too much line. The further and deeper she went, the more chance there would be of the line catching on some of the submerged stalks and bushes. She kept kicking her tail, with me not giving her any line and turning her over on her back. By this time a friend, Grant, had come over and was on hand with the net. He knew which fish it was, I knew which fish it was, and neither of us said a word until I'd steered her towards the net and he'd lifted the mesh around her.

PB Common

She was huge, and although I'd never seen her on the bank or in the water, Grant was an Arena veteran and even he remarked how big she looked. I bit the line, and as she was lying in the net.

We weighed her at 36lb 8oz, a personal-best common by a few pounds, and she looked absolutely immense, a real good armful of carp. She was my biggest maggot-caught Arena carp by some margin, and on a day when everything was pointing towards a frustrating blank. Carp angling fortunes really do change in an instant.

It was one of the last Arena carp I caught before almost every one of the lake's carp died later that year following a stocking of new fish. Dwelling on the fatalities and heartache only serves to remember the carp in their darkest hour, not their finest. They are gone but, to me, will never be forgotten.

The Carp Fishing Jigsaw

There are many pieces to the jigsaw that is carp fishing and every now and then they all fall into place. Dave Levy tells the story of when his did exactly that...

I've always seen fishing for big carp a bit like putting a jigsaw puzzle together; you need all the pieces to get the full picture and even then a bit of luck is still needed.

It was one of those days that we carp anglers just love to be out fishing – low pressure, cloudy and a strong southwesterly wind blowing up. What more could you want?

I was sat staring out of the window at work, not where I wanted to be on a day like this at all. How could I get out early? Think Levy, think! No, it's no good, I'd already had food poisoning three times this year, my wife has now had more kids than a spider and the brother I never had, had passed away and come back to life so many times that my boss now thinks he is called Lazarus. Oh well, looks as though I'll have to wait until six o'clock!

By the time I got out of work the sky was starting to look very stormy as thick black clouds masked the horizon: "Looks like rain," I thought. My trusty van had been loaded up with all my tackle that morning and was now flying doing the motorway at the speed of sound (ahem), in a bid to get me to the lake in time to set up before the rain came.

Fish Spotting

As soon as I got to the lake the rods and gear were pulled out and chucked on to the carp barrow in double-quick time. I approached the lake and could see that the weed had really come up since the last time I'd looked around. I dropped my barrow in the first swim and had a walk around to see if I could find any carp. Although it wasn't fish-spotting weather, the water was so gin clear I thought that I might just see something worth moving on to. It wasn't until I got to the back of where the wind was blowing that I saw two good carp moving slowly down the side of a weed bed. I watched them until they moved out of sight, some 20 or so yards away. This was where the weed became really thick. I didn't need telling twice – that would do just fine.

My excuses ran dry: I'd had food poisoning three times and my wife had had more kids than a spider. At work 'til six o'clock then!

Confidence in a bag.

I quickly shot around and got my tackle. There were two swims that I could reach this area of the lake from, but the one closest to the big weed bed gave me a much better line angle. From here I could cast against the weed bed, rather than over it. The only problem was I'd be much closer to the spots I would be fishing. I set my Groundhog brolly up as far back as I could, so as to remain largely out of sight. I then put the banksticks in with the minimum of fuss and noise. I didn't want to use a marker if the two big fish were still about as I didn't want to risk spooking them.

I cast the first bait to a clear patch off the corner of an island. The area was about four feet deep with a shining gold, clay strip petering away into deeper water. I PVA'd two pop-ups on to my hook bait in the hope that they would keep my bait suspended long enough for me to pull back the rig to the edge of the clear spot. I baited up by catapulting 20 or so Nash Tangee Peach boilies out around the area. My cast landed perfectly and the pop-ups did their job before the PVA melted and they rose to the surface – perfect!

I had set up my second rod with the new Trigger Link. The hook link was fairly longish, about 12 inches, with a size 6 Fang-X wide-gaped hook tied on line-aligner style. The bait was a 15mm Tangee Peach, an all-time favourite of mine and one that has caught me loads of carp.

In The Weed

I decided that this bait would be cast right in to the thick of the weed, with a large, drawstring PVA bag on it. This is a method that a lot of anglers don't know, but one which is so good to use on weedy waters. It can be really effective if you have the confidence to try it.

I could just make out the really thick weed below the surface; I unclipped the hook link, so I just had the lead on, and I then dropped the lead in alongside the weed. On pulling back I could feel it was a lot thinner here. I clipped it up to mark for my next cast. I put the hook link back on, which now had the large bag of broken baits and small pellets attached. When I cast out it hit the water like a bouncing bomb but right on target. When fishing in weed I always let the end tackle

Baits out, traps set and wait.

Many anglers would be put off by this sight.

drop straight to the bottom. If you hold it on a tight line it tends to pick up more weed on the way down, masking the presentation.

I put another 100 or so baits over the weed rod, as close as I could to the hook bait, so there was a nice little pile of food among the weed – that's if they wanted it.

I really felt as though all the jigsaw pieces were there, I just hoped they were all in the right place.

I sat back and put the kettle on and, even though the sky was still dark, no rain had fallen while I was setting up, which was a bit of luck. My friend Gary turned up for a chat and a cupper and we talked for a few hours about all things carpy. During this time three good carp rolled in and around the thick weed bed. There looked to be some good old-fashioned bubbling up going on out there too. I hoped that this was carp rooting around for my freebies and, ultimately, my hook bait. I was on edge looking at the bobbins, hoping one would fly up at any moment. After a while Gary said his goodbyes and I was left sitting alone once again. I sat at the water's edge listening to an owl that was hooting loudly in the nearby woods. Non-anglers rarely experience such moments and it is great to just soak them up sometimes. It had been a long day so I climbed, reluctantly, into my sleeping bag.

It was about 11.30pm that I heard the first tip tapping of rain on my brolly, then, over the next 20 minutes, it turned into a downpour. I had to put all my bits and pieces to the back of the brolly to stop them getting wet, as the wind was picking up and blowing rain into the front of my 'house'. I started to think that maybe the wife was right – I am mad sitting out in this weather under a little green shelter! At some point in between the wind and rain I fell back to sleep.

Realtree Bikini

I was just in the middle of a pukka dream where Kate Moss was in a Realtree bikini and weighing Two Tone for me at a new British record of 70lb, when I was woken by a few bleeps on one of the alarms. It was just as well that I woke up because Kate would have only got the hump when she saw me cuddling the carp and not her!

It was the weed rod that had received a liner. I sat up and looked hard to see beyond the bright, blue light from my buzzer, the bullet braid still hung slack in the rod's eyes. I looked at my watch; it was 2.15am. I couldn't get back to sleep after that, so I put the kettle on.

The rain started to ease off, until it eventually stopped. I looked out onto the now flat-calm lake just in time to see a dark shape roll and a few minutes later another one showed right over the bait! I wasn't sure if it was the same carp because there were only 20-odd in the pond. Over the next 20 minutes I saw 10 more rolls, although still no bites. Something must be wrong, I thought. Maybe the weed was just too thick in that spot for them to find the hook bait. Even

"I was in the middle of a dream where Kate Moss was in a Realtree bikini, weighing Two Tone for me at 70lb..."

Pukka!

Slack lines – perfect.

A wonderful sight.

One last shot.

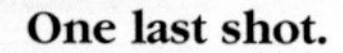

worse, my rig could be tangled. These thoughts are not nice and often accompany a biteless period, when you know fish are present in the swim. I was getting myself into a right state, when suddenly the bobbin on the weed rod lifted up slowly to the alarm. I was on it in a shot, hovering over the rod in anticipation of it flying off. The bobbin just sat against the alarm. I slackened the braid and the bobbin was back down where it had been. Liner maybe? I had just turned to walk away when the bobbin hit the alarm with a crack! The alarm let rip, breaking the night's silence.

I grabbed the rod and bent into a carp, I was helpless as the rod just took on its full curve as the carp punched its way through the big weed bed, ripping line from the spool. Suddenly it all came to an abrupt halt.

Locked Up

I applied a bit more pressure but nothing was giving – the fish was locked up solid in the weed. It had now started to pour down with rain again and I was soaked through, so after a few minutes I put the rod down on to the rest on a tight line. I never like playing out loads of slack to a weeded fish. With a tight line, as the carp starts to kick its head round the line, it turns them the right way around.

I was starting to wonder if maybe the carp had gone and left my hook lodged in the weed. I then told myself to be patient. It can sometimes take a very long time for the fish to make its way out of such a situation, so all may not yet be lost, I thought.

I made a fresh cup of tea and took off my wet clothes. After a good 20 minutes, and with me sitting in just my pants and T-shirt, trying to dry my socks, the rod tip started bouncing. I walked over and leant into the rod, this time I was gaining line straightaway. I could feel the braid grating on the weed as the carp kicked its way through. It broke the surface 10 yards out, sending large ripples to the bank.

I was now soaked from head to toe again, as the rain continued to pour down. Every now and then all carp anglers ask themselves why they are there, but with a decent carp

"I was soaked as the rain continued to pour down. It was one of those moments when you question why you are there."

"I applied a bit more steady pressure but nothing was happening. The fish was locked up solid in the weed."

"Please stay on, please!"

on the end of my line I knew exactly why.

As the carp powered off to my right, taking more line, a big bow wave broke the water in front of it – at least it was now going away from the weed bed. For the next five minutes I played a very angry carp, as twice more he tried to make the weed and rolled on the surface just short of the danger zone. My nerves were shot to bits – big carp that fight really hard put years on me and I knew this was a very large carp. Now, it looked as though I had him beaten, he was wallowing just a few feet out. Slowly, he came over the

> **"I got into the lake and, as soon as I opened the weigh sling, the carp waddled strongly away and disappeared."**

net cord and I could see the bulk of the carp as his nose touched the spreader block and I lifted the net. He was mine.

I sat back on the wet grass; rain still pouring down on my face, looked at the sky and shouted: "COME ON! – Bring it on because I no longer give a sh*t." I pulled myself together and sorted out the unhooking mat, scales and sling. Once the scales were zeroed, I rolled the net up and carried the big carp to the mat where I carefully layed him down. I unrolled the net and there, in the first light of day, was a long, solid-looking carp, almost black in colour – a pure beast.

The hook had fallen out in the net so I just pushed the weighing sling under him, making sure all the fins were flat. I then hooked the scales onto the sling and lifted him up. The needle went round into the forties and came to a slow halt around 48 to 49lb – I settled for 48lb 12oz.

Dawn Chorus

I'll tell you what – we carp anglers may be mad, but mad can feel bloody great sometimes! I put him in a carp sack and staked it out in some deep water, where no harm could come to him. I sat down under my brolly and turned my stove on full to dry myself out. A short while later the rain stopped and the birds sounded the dawn chorus. I soaked it all up – a very contented carp angler.

I called a friend, Lee, who kindly came down and took some cracking photos, for which I am eternally grateful. I told Lee all about my eventful night. He'd been fast a sleep at home and hadn't even heard it raining.

It was now time to release my prize back to his watery home. I got into the lake and opened the weigh sling. As soon as water

They weren't too shy.

flooded over the carp it strongly waddled away, disappearing back in to the thick green weed from where he'd been so rudely pulled only hours before.

I reeled the rods in and took a slow walk to the van. After chucking all my wet tackle in the back I got in and started the engine. It was at this point the radio turned on. It was Heart FM and the tune playing was Phil Collins' I Wish it Would Rain Down On Me. Bizarre.

As I switched off, I reflected on another completed jigsaw. However, there'll always be others and my thoughts soon turned to my next, Conningbrook, and the hunt for that record carp. Kate Moss or no Kate Moss, I knew I'd be giving it my best shot.

Another part of the carp fishing jigsaw complete – I was a very happy man.

So it's snowing – you can't let a little thing like that put you off, can you?

The Sixth Sense

Anglers at the top of carp fishing are often credited with a sixth sense that helps them catch fish. Paul Forward recalls four of his most memorable carp fishing exploits, each of which would back this theory up...

Just one of the stunning carp I was blessed with on the first day at the Herts club water.

In the close season of 1993, I managed to acquire a much sought-after ticket for a 50-acre, no publicity, Herefordshire club water. I was absolutely bubbling with excitement at the prospect of fishing there. By the time June 15th came around I was raring to go. I'd fished the water as a guest a couple of times with Lee Jackson and Dave Woods and I thought it was the most fantastic-looking lake I'd ever seen. It was surrounded with majestic, mature trees and boasted big, open expanses of water, with huge gravel bars, islands, shallow bays, lilies and weed. All this and some of the best looking and largest carp in the land – heaven indeed!

Over the next few weeks I chatted endlessly with Lee about tactics, swim choice, which bait to use and all those things that carp anglers discuss before a campaign.

Over the previous few seasons I'd been catching loads of fish everywhere during the warmer months on hemp and tiger nuts, and I was feeling very confident that I could catch carp anywhere employing similar tactics. The two basic requirements to make this method really work well were plenty of weed and some carp but neither of these could be guaranteed! Let me explain. First of all, it being opening day of the season, there would be the usual draw for swims and with around 40 anglers turning up the odds of getting on fish were not good, even if I did have any idea where they might be, which I didn't. I decided my best bet would be to have no particular swim in mind, but just to try and get into one of the heavily weeded island swims. Here, I would be able to utilise my hemp-and-tigers approach to its best effect. I'd also decided to take along a couple of kilos of my special, home-made boilies, just in case I had to fish further out in one of the more open areas of the lake.

The draw was held around 7pm, in the club car park, the evening before the season opened. I drew 15, which meant 15th choice of swim, not too bad. As the anglers before me chose their swims I began to panic. Then on the map of the lake in front of us a swim named The Forty Two caught my eye. Lee confirmed that it was at the end of the islands and weedy. "That'll do," I thought and, when my turn arrived, this is what I chose.

We were allowed to start fishing at 4am. No night fishing is allowed on this water nor was baiting up. So, with nothing more to be done, it was off to the Whip & Collar pub for a meal, a few jars of beer and some good old fishing banter. The inevitable overindulgence occurred and Woodsy, Alan, Steve, Lee and myself, and a few others, sang all the way back to camp in the car park about midnight. So much for having an early night!

> **The alarm clocks were ringing and carp anglers were scurrying off to their swims, laden with tackle. At the time I was the only one with a wheelbarrow, they just weren't fashionable yet, so rapid progress saw me make my way to the '40s'.**

Ready For 'The Off'

All too soon the alarm clocks were ringing and carp anglers were scurrying off to their swims, laden with tackle. At the time, I was the only angler with a wheelbarrow, they just weren't fashionable yet, so rapid progress was made and a few minutes later I found myself in The Forty Two. The lake here is about 100 yards wide, with a long, narrow island dividing it just about centrally. The island is covered in fully-grown trees, so the other side of the lake is completely obscured. It was about 40 yards to the island and to my amazement there were one or two fish about. There was thick marginal weed for about one and a half to two rod lengths and more weed on a bar two-thirds of the way across. It was definitely no place for a marker float, as it would scare the fish already there.

Over the last couple of seasons I'd taught myself how to 'donk' (feel the lead drop and hit the bottom). This gave me a lot of confidence when fishing in the weed. A large willow, overhanging the margin 20 yards down the bank looked an obvious place for my first rod. I was using 18lb Maxima; 1½oz leads, semi-fixed onto the rig tubing with two inches of silicone tubing; 15lb hook link and a size 4 Drennan hook with two balanced tigers as hook baits.

My first cast, about three feet from the edge of the weed, nearly clipped the leaves of the overhanging tree and as the lead hit the bottom I felt a nice, solid 'donk' – perfect. I put the rod in the rest and walked down the bank to the tree and catapulted six pints of hempseed fairly tightly around my hook

bait, followed by two pouches of tiger nuts, job done.

I could see fish vortexing and occasionally rolling on the bar and after a couple of casts with exactly the same tackle as the other rod, I found what I was looking for, a small clear area in between the weed beds. I fired two pouches of tigers around the hook bait and sat down for a brew, it was now 4.20am. I had both rods out and I was pretty happy with each.

To be honest, because it was my very first day as a member, I didn't know what to expect. I had been told that it was a pretty hard lake, but the rewards could be worth it. Some of the top anglers had boasted 10 or more fish per season.

I'd also been told that the carp were very fussy about bait and that my plan of hemp and tigers had been tried before with little success. However, I was buzzing with confidence and excitement. As I finished my last slurp of tea the rod on the bar melted off, just as my good mate John Baker was passing on route to his swim. After a short but spirited scrap I landed my first carp of the season, a perfect mirror of about 18lb.

"As I finished my last slurp of tea the rod on the bar melted off, just as my good mate John Baker was passing on route to his swim. I soon landed my first carp of the season, a perfect mirror of about 18lb."

"Wow," I thought, it's always a relief to get the first one, but now I wanted some more! The bait was still okay so out it went again, followed by another two pouches of nuts. The same rod was off again 10 minutes later. This time it was a lovely dark common of just over 20lb. What a start!

Away Again

I checked the hook and bait and cast back in the same spot, put the rod on the rest, clipped the bobbin on and was just about to sit down when I was away again; this time a mirror of 16lb. I couldn't believe my luck, three fish and it was still only 5am. I rang Jacko and told him of my good fortune, he said: "Well done mate. You never know, you might even have some more." Lee informed me that no other carp had been caught yet. Then, suddenly, the right-hand rod, which up until now I'd almost forgotten about, roared off.

After a few moments I got the feeling that this was a much better fish and I begrudgingly had to give line against its powerful surges. The fish was trying hard to get into the heavy weed in the near margin, and every time I'd just managed to hang on by leaning out and applying heavy side strain with the rod bent double. It was touch and go, but each time I just about managed to slow it down and turn it around, only for a repeat performance. This one was trying to pull my arms out of their sockets! It must have been 10 minutes before I saw it roll on the surface, nearly reaching the sanctuary of the weed again, but I could definitely feel it tiring, the same of which could have been said about me. A few moments later I slowly drew it over the net and let out a sigh of relief. I was stunned at the size, shape and condition of this fish, it looked like it had been on steroids and weight-training every day; it was so muscular and powerful looking. I slipped it in the sling and carefully placed him (I'd decided it must be a he) into the margins. I telephoned Woodsy and told him the news. He thought I was winding him up at first but after a while I convinced him I was telling the truth and persuaded him to wind in his rods and come and take some photos.

On the scales it was a fraction over 38lb and absolutely magnificent. Woodsy departed, remarking that I was indeed a jammy bugger. I rebaited and recast both rods on the same spots. It was still only 6am.

That first-day trip to the Herts club water proved to be beyond my wildest dreams. I'd caught as many as some can in a season and I felt truly privileged. The hemp and tiger nuts had, despite the advice I'd been given, done the business.

Two At Once

Another 20 minutes had passed when I saw small patches of bubbles appearing on the surface, close to the margin bait. Some more bubbles burst the surface and then, suddenly, the rod tip pulled right round and I was in again. This one made the sanctuary of the weed on its first run, but with steady pressure I managed to coax the fish, plus a bale of weed, to come free. It was while I was heaving this mass towards me that the other rod roared off! "Oh ****," I thought – not very good timing. With nobody to assist, I decided to try and ignore the second rod and deal with the first one as quickly as possible. Luck was again on my side and, with the weed covering its head, this fish allowed itself to be eased straight into the landing net.

When I'd made sure I had the weed-covered fish in the net, I put my foot on the net handle to secure it and picked up the other rod. This one had travelled about 20 yards and stopped. At first I thought it may have dropped off in the weed, but after pulling for a few seconds it decided to pull back and, with a kick of its tail, came out of

The Thick Head fish from the awesome Savay. Fate and circumstances were really playing a part in my captures by now.

"It was while I was reeling the mass of fish and weed towards me that the other rod roared off. "Oh **," I thought – not very good timing. With nobody to assist I had to ignore it!"**

the weed. When your luck is in, everything goes right, and this one didn't put up much of a scrap either, with weed again covering its head. "Now for the tricky bit," I thought. The net was already very heavy with one carp and the weed in it, making it impossible to manoeuvre. I had an idea. I put the net handle onto my knee, so that it dipped the net cord, wound down hard with my reel and then heaved the fish across the surface and straight into the net first time. It worked like a dream. Phew! I needed a ciggy. I rang Woodsy and told him of my epic drama. "I don't believe you F," he said, adding that he'd be along in a minute.

I held the fish in the net until Dave arrived and a lovely brace they were too, a dark, heavily scaled mirror of 27lb 12oz and a dark common of 22lb. I thanked Dave for his help and he walked back to his swim shaking his head. Nobody else had had any action!

I didn't think that it could carry on much longer and was certain that the fish would move off. However, at about 7.30am I caught another low-twenty mirror on the rod on the bar. This time they did leave the swim, but I didn't exactly complain.

I fished on until 10.30pm without a sign of another fish. They'd moved to the far end of the lake where Lee Jackson had caught three or four fish that afternoon. With there being no night fishing allowed, I returned to the same spot at 4am hoping for a repeat performance, but I didn't even see a carp. I fished the same swim many more times over the following seasons and never had a single bite from it! When I look back on my seven-fish catch it makes me realise now just how fortunate I was on that opening day in 1993.

I'd now like to tell you of yet another tale of the unexpected and unforeseen, that revolved around opening day a few years afterwards.

All the usual suspects, including Lockey, Jacko, Alan Partridge, Steve, Alan Parsons, Jim Burns, Woodsy, myself and many more, had again arrived the evening before the season opened for the eagerly awaited swim draw at the Colne Valley water. With my greater knowledge of the water I had chosen three or four possible swims. However, I pulled out number 41, meaning that I would just about be the last angler to choose a swim. I stayed just in case one of my favoured pegs wouldn't be chosen, but alas, one by one, they were taken and my heart sank.

I'd also managed to get a place on the Looney Rota at Savay the year before, after three or four years of fishing the water on a day-only season ticket. So, after wishing good luck to all my mates, I jumped back in the van and drove the three miles up the road to Savay.

Stitched Up

I'd missed the draw by a couple of hours, so the rest of the rota had already settled into their swims and, as fishing was allowed to commence straight after the draw, most were already off and running. I loaded up my barrow and set off for the long walk ahead. The Cottage Bay was already taken, so were all the swims in the North Bay that I'd quite fancied. I set off down the canal bank, Andy's and the Reeds were taken and someone was in the Logs and the Gravelly. The next swim, the Brambles, was free and, would you believe it, a few fish were showing at about 90 yards, slightly to the right. The next swim down was the Birches and one of the Swindon lads was fishing there but that was quite a long way off, so I thought I would give it a go where I'd seen the fish. I quickly set up my three rods with 3oz leads, 4in hooklengths and 20 bottom baits – my home-made specials! I always preferred to make all my own base mixes in my lock-up garage, which I converted into a small bait factory, researching and obtaining the finest ingredients. This way, I could also guarantee the freshness of the ingredients, and this gave me 100 per cent confidence in my bait (this same base mix is now sold by my good mate Lockey at Solar and is called 'Club Mix').

I cast the first rod out about 90 yards to the left-hand edge of where the fish were showing and felt it land nicely. I cast the middle rod about 100 yards and straight out, again on the fringes of where the fish were showing. The lead landed with a nice 'donk' as it hit a firm bottom. With a throwing stick I was able to scatter a few baits in the general area. I didn't want to overdo the casting or baiting and spook all of them, so I was pretty pleased with both rods.

It was around 9pm and the light was fading quickly. I decided not to risk another cast near the fish with my right-hand rod and flicked it down the margin with a pouchful of boilies following behind it. Job done. Up went the brolly and bedchair and I cracked open a can of beer! It was a lovely, warm, still evening and even though I was ready for a sit down, I decided to pop down to the chap in the Birches and offer him a beer to celebrate the beginning of the new season and all that. I rarely need an excuse! I'd taken about 10 steps in his direction when I heard a buzzer cry out; it took a

Breathtaking. And to think, I should have been meeting the boys in the pub!

"Tony suggested I have a go and, as I had a couple of hours to spare, I thought that it would be silly not to! I hurried back to the van and grabbed my rods and a few bits of tackle and wandered around the other side of the shallows."

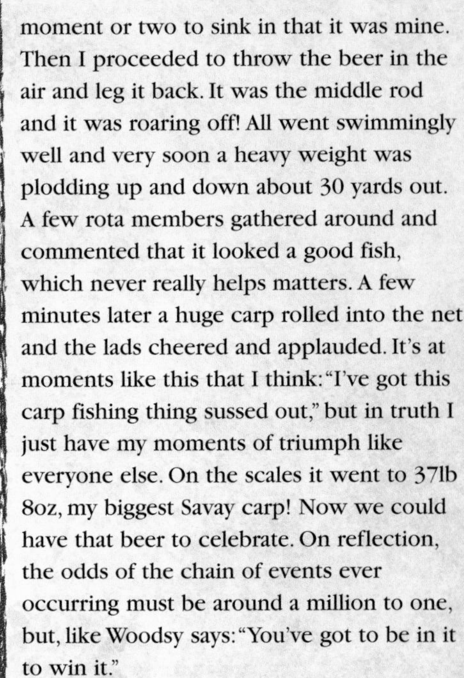

moment or two to sink in that it was mine. Then I proceeded to throw the beer in the air and leg it back. It was the middle rod and it was roaring off! All went swimmingly well and very soon a heavy weight was plodding up and down about 30 yards out. A few rota members gathered around and commented that it looked a good fish, which never really helps matters. A few minutes later a huge carp rolled into the net and the lads cheered and applauded. It's at moments like this that I think: "I've got this carp fishing thing sussed out," but in truth I just have my moments of triumph like everyone else. On the scales it went to 37lb 8oz, my biggest Savay carp! Now we could have that beer to celebrate. On reflection, the odds of the chain of events ever occurring must be around a million to one, but, like Woodsy says: "You've got to be in it to win it."

On another occasion I had arranged to meet Roger Smith, Kerry and Lockey in the Horse and Barge, prior to a session at Savay. We'd arranged to meet around 7pm, have a swift half, some food and then commence our session. I finished my work around midday so, after packing my gear, I was off up the M25 at around 1.30pm. It would be a good thing to be there early, as it would give me chance to have a good look around the lake prior to fishing and maybe give me a few clues as to where to fish. From past experience, I knew all too well what a swift half in the pub could lead to.

The Shallows

Anyway, as I approached Junction 17, I decided that a quick look at another Colne Valley water would be a good idea. I could see my good friend Tony Hall's truck in the car park when I pulled in, so I wandered off to find him and have a chat and a brew. Tony was in a shallow bay not far away and the kettle was on straightaway. He informed me that the lake was fishing quite well and at this very moment there were a few good fish in the shallows. Tony suggested that I should have a go and, as I had a couple of hours to spare, I thought that it would be silly not to! I hurried back to the van and grabbed a couple of rods and a few bits of tackle and wandered around the other side of the shallows. It was very hot and humid and, with no breeze at all, it was almost unbearably sweaty. I decided to fish a small reedy point at the furthest end of the shallows. The water here was only about two to three feet deep but I had fished it a few times before and felt I knew it quiet well. The bay was solid with weed and, to make matters worse, on top of this was an almost impenetrable crust of thick, pea-green blanket weed.

I cast a 1½oz lead into a few likely looking gaps in the weed and after a couple of casts found the little 'donks' that indicated a clearish bottom. I fired a couple of pouches of my home-made boilies tightly around both of the rods and sat down, pleased with my efforts. About a quarter of an hour later, big, dark, ominous-looking clouds gathered, and the skies turned black – then the thunder came. I was beginning to have second thoughts about this impromptu session. The inevitable rain came down in torrents and I huddled under my small brolly thinking that this was one of my worst decisions ever. Then the rain stopped and the clouds cleared, leaving a misty heat. In a remarkable turnaround, I could make out a few fish around my baits. On the right-hand spot bubbles and vortexes broke the surface. I knelt next to the rod and a few seconds later the water erupted and the buzzer screamed out. Even though I was on it straightaway, it took enough line to get into the weed and I just hung on. The fish kept moving through and I gained a few feet at a time. The blanket weed was getting stuck fast in the tip ring and twice I had to put the rod down and clear it, each time expecting the hook to fall out. Now I had the fish, plus a ton of weed, about a rod length out, and solid weed between the fish and me – it wasn't going to be easy. As nobody was near enough to help out, I devised a plan. I sunk the net in the margin, tightened down with the clutch and walked backwards. The line sang under the tension before the whole lot started moving towards me. I continued walking back until I saw the rig tube over the net. I quickly dropped the rod and grabbed the line just in front of the tubing and hoisted the fish, and the weed bed, into the net. Not entirely conventional I know, but it had worked.

A mid-twenty on the social at Chilham. I just knew I should be somewhere else though and was soon doing the off.

"It was early January, if I remember correctly, but it felt more like autumn. Overcast skies and southwesterly winds and temperatures up to 13 or 14°C – perfect conditons for catching carp."

As I started clearing the weed it became clear that it was indeed a very big fish that I had landed. It was massive, with huge shoulders and a wrist wider than any I've ever seen. I called Tony over and we weighed and photographed a truly magnificent carp at 47lb, which at the time was the largest fish in the lake. The whole series of events was truly unbelievable and unexpected. I decided that was enough excitement for one day and packed my rods away and set off to the Horse and Barge to meet the boys. I couldn't wait to tell them my story.

My final tale is of an instinct or feeling we carp anglers sometimes get. It's hard to explain what it is, maybe a sixth sense. Whatever it is, I wish it would happen more often. Anyway, it was during the winter of 2001 that myself and a few of the Conningbrook regulars, including Pet Food Paul and Simon, decided on a social bit of angling at one of the Chilham Mill waters, Stour Lake. It was early January if I remember correctly but it felt like autumn, with strong southwesterly winds, overcast skies and temperatures up to 13 or14°C – excellent carp-catching conditions. I set up mid-afternoon on the back of the wind, after seeing two fish roll at that end of the lake. During the next hour I saw several more fish in my baited area, then, sure enough, I was in to my first carp of the year, an unusual-looking mirror of about 18lb and very welcome indeed. During the evening we chatted and enjoyed an Indian takeaway.

Conditions were perfect. Shortly after getting in the bag I was disturbed by another mirror carp of a similar size to the first and after this capture I could not sleep.

Colne Valley Journey

My thoughts were full of visions of the Colne Valley lake and the swim where I had caught a 32-pounder just before Christmas. Would they still be there? The more I thought about it, the more unsettled I became. At 4am, in the pitch black, I could rest no more. I swiftly packed up my gear, pushed the barrow back to the van and set off on the 100-mile journey to the Colne Valley.

There was no need to hurry, as fishing wasn't allowed until 6am. I arrived to find I was the only one there. This was great news, as I could get in the swim I wanted. I had a new rig, the '360 rig' that my good friend Dave Lane had told me about, and was keen to try it out. I put it on two of my three rods with a small orange pop-up and cast them both towards the area I had caught from on the previous trip. The third rod went on another favourite spot of mine. The wind carried on pushing from the southwest and it was still unseasonably mild. I was fishing at very long range and over a number of steep gravel banks, so I was using a semi-sinking braid to keep the line high and very tight. At 9am the left-hand bobbin dropped to the floor and shot up again. Following a spirited tussle, I landed a pretty 19-pounder. I thought: "This rig works okay," and put it back out again. A quarter of an hour later and the same rod, same thing, only a much better fish by the feel of it. After a few nervous moments when I picked up the line on the middle rod, I managed to get the fish over the last bar and plodding up and down the margins. Five minutes later and she was mine. What a beauty - 40lb 4oz in all its winter splendour.

I cast both rods back out to the same spots and five minutes later I had another take, but unfortunately the hook pulled after just a few seconds

Three takes in 45 minutes on a very difficult water in mid-winter, after packing up at 4am and driving 100 miles from fishing a lake in Kent, and all because of a gut feeling that I had. I cannot really explain what it is, but I like to think it is a glimpse of some sort of sixth sense, what else could it be? Surely it couldn't just be luck?

So, my tales end, or at least these ones. I have experiance this strange phenomena on many occasions and have read and talked about it with other anglers even more.

I don't know whether carp anglers have a sixth sense. It might sound a bit strange, but I cannot discount it from my thoughts.

The early season hit, my decision to leave a busy water and travel to Savay, the chance encounter with my mate on the Colne Valley water and the 'calling' back to the scene of a previous success, despite the ordeal of getting there - all of these stories had something behind there occasion.

I could easily have stayed at Chilham and enjoyed the social, but the feeling inside me to be somewhere else was so strong that I could not ignore it.

Sixth sense, carp gods, coincidence or sheer luck? I don't know what it is, but I sure well know it exists.

"Three takes in 45 minutes on a very difficult water in mid-winter and after packing up at 4am and driving 100 miles from a lake in Kent. All because of a gut feeling that I had. I cannot really explain what it is – maybe a sixth sense?"

I just knew I had to be there. Had I not made the effort I would not have been blessed with this glorious winter carp.

A full moon on a balmy autumn evening and expectations are high.

FROM AN UNDISCLOSED NORTHERN STILLWATER...

They're secret squirrels up in the northwest of England and many catch reports are followed by captions reading 'caught from an undisclosed northwest stillwater'. Neil Smith tells of one such water that brought him a most memorable capture...

I am a firm believer in fate, not only throughout life but also within angling. Being there at the right time is the single ingredient that cannot be bought off the shelf. Not only did fate play its part in the final capture of an incredible creature, one that had not graced the banks for many a year, but also in me finding myself on the banks of one of Cheshire's true 'undisclosed northwest stillwaters' in the first place.

Characters And Friends

Working in a tackle shop brings you into contact with all manner of characters. In time these characters become friends and confidants, with many sharing with you secret baits, methods and, of course, waters. There are times when many of these secrets, especially the ones relating to large carp or pike, are more fiction than fact. The amount of white elephants you can be fed are numerous - a big carp to the matchman or pleasure guy may not necessarily be a large carp to you or I.

During the winter period of 1997 an irresistible offer came my way from a guy who has since become a very good friend. As I said, the characters visiting the shop were numerous, with Jeff being one of them. Jeff Hook! I did think his name was a wind-up at first but, nevertheless, the offer was there for a day's pike fishing on a private Cheshire mere, one that, at the time, only he had access to fish during winter.

We arrived in the dark and as dawn broke so did the tranquillity and beauty of the lake. It was set within the grounds of an 18th century Gothic castle. The castle overlooked one end of the lake, with a dense wood at the end we fished from. Atmospheric it most definitely was!

Colin, the gamekeeper, arrived to collect his money. As is often the case with these characters he turned out to be quite an eccentric. Brandishing a double-barreled shotgun, he told us he was looking for a Canada goose that he had recently shot for the pot!

He had those eyes that looked in two directions at the same time; look northwest, if you know what I mean. This made conversation hard, as you didn't know which one to talk to. Plus, it gave the impression that he was looking at something behind you. But what came out in this riddle of a conversation set up a slice of what has since turned out to be northwest carp fishing history. The conversation went like this:

"Fabulous place you have here Colin. How long have you worked the estate?" I asked.

"All mi life, with mi father before mi," came the reply.

"Is it right there's some good bream running into double figures in here, as well as tench?" I continued.

"Aye, and some big carp."

I was stunned into a silence.

It took a second or two for that last sentence to sink in. Jeff had fished more in winter with odd trips during summer for tench, with no mention of carp. The other anglers that could fish during summer were targeting bream - the lake was situated in the heart of Cheshire bream territory - and this had attracted a who's who of bream angling.

Once I composed myself and had gone around the houses, purposely avoiding the mention of carp, so as not to give away my hunger for more info, I posed the question: "You mentioned carp, Colin. With the bream so large what size do the carp go to?"

"Dunno, no-one bothers with 'em. The Ladyship (from the castle) wanted them moving from one of the other pools on the estate as they were colouring the water up. We moved them over here some years ago. Couldn't find containers large enough for some of 'em."

I asked what the availability of tickets was and when the season started. Luckily there were two tickets up for grabs from a possible 30. I quickly left the name of a friend as well as my own.

Closed Shop

Our luck was in as, some months later, Peter Hodkinson and myself gained access to what turned out to be quite a closed shop. I wasn't sure what sort of reception I would receive from the other members once they realised that I was there for the carp. It was mixed, with one member telling me that I was wasting my time here because there were no carp in the lake. I had since tried to get an exact figure from Colin, who estimated it to be as many as 50.

The mere spanned some 12 to 14 acres, with the wood being at the southern end where I had spent my winter's days pike

A richly deserved capture. Jeff Hook with the fish that was later nicknamed Broad Bean, after the bait that he caught it on.

"He had those eyes that looked in two directions at the same time; look northwest, if you know what I mean! It gave the impression that he was looking at something behind you. What he told us though set up what was to become Cheshire carp fishing history."

The bream were monsters and us carp anglers were not always made welcome by the syndicate that fished for them.

Looking out over the northwest stillwater. We didn't know exactly what was in there, but we knew there were some nice carp.

> I shinned back up the tree once more. The light was fading but I could see that the water had cleared and my chance was gone. It looked like this could be a spot for the day, with the fish leaving at night.

fishing. This end boasted two bays, with an island that had a wooden jetty to fish from. The view from the island was incredible, with 95 per cent of the lake visible and the castle as the backdrop. This end was relatively deep, in excess of 10 feet in places, with a fairly uniform bottom. The opposite end, that received the southerly winds, was much shallower, with a ledge that ran all the way along the east bank. The mere at this end tapered off, running under a bridge into a very shallow pool.

Breathless

It was in this back pool that Jeff and Peter first spotted a fish in early May. Having received two breathless phone calls from them, both regarding the sighting of an extremely long common from the bridge, I left home for my usual Sunday-night session. Neither wanted to put a weight on the fish but both agreed it to be well over 30lb. On arrival, I shinned up a tree further down the small pool, under the bridge. Once up there I could see the usually gin-clear water was coloured. The light wasn't great as it was well after 6pm, the time when you could access the estate on a Sunday. In among the coloured water I could just make out a tail wafting through the plumes of silt.

The area that the fish were feeding in was difficult to present a bait - beneath an overhanging tree with a bed of rushes in front of me. I decided, due to the shallowness of the water and the deep silt, to practically freeline with no lead on the clip. Before I swung it out I shinned the tree again. The water had cleared somewhat with no sign of the fish. I slid down and swung out a couple of grains of corn. I pushed the rod down into the base of the rushes, with the tip into the silt so as to conceal the main line.

Time ticked by with no signs of activity. I still needed to set up for the night with all but this rod and net still in the van. I shinned back up the tree once more. The light was fading but I could see that the water was clear and my chance had gone. It looked like this could well be a spot for the day, with the fish moving back out under the bridge into the main lake for the night. I dropped some hemp, corn, boilies and peanuts on to the spot, hoping that they and I would return tomorrow.

First Sighting

The night, as the previous few nights that I had fished, was quiet. The occasional bream rolled early on but the carp were nowhere to be seen. It was becoming clear that there were only a few fish present in the mere and that Colin's 50 may be a bit over the top. Having got to know a few of the locals I was let into the secret that, since the introduction of the carp from the other pool, the bream guys had taken it upon themselves to 'relocate' any that were caught, even describing the carp as 'vermin'.

The following day I did get to clearly see my first carp, a mirror that looked to be around mid-twenty. It was on its own as it waddled under the bridge. I hoped this was the first of a few. The spot that I baited had been cleared, not by carp though, but by swans. This shallow backwater was a nightmare to fish, with resident nesting swans, deep silt and practically no access. The mirror waddled back out under the bridge, turning right and out into the main lake. Shortly afterwards, two commons entered the pool. I followed them on foot until they laid up along some Norfolk reed. Never once did they look to feed. I needed to find the spots out in the main lake where the fish fed.

The use of boats for baiting up was allowed and the need for one was a must if I was to locate what was turning out to be a small number of carp; fish that hardly ever received angling pressure and were probably set into a undisturbed daily routine. I found a fibreglass dinghy for sale in the local Loot magazine. After a bit of repair work and some camouflage paint, it was soon ready to go.

Due to commitments on various other waters, and the small matter of getting hitched in August, I didn't get to return until the back end of September. On my return, a weed bed had emerged halfway along the east bank, sitting on top of the drop-off. I could wade with chesties to the back, where I could make out holes that appeared to be clear in the centre.

The boat had been moored up for over a month and had a large amount of water slopping around inside, so the first job was to bail this out. I stepped aboard and, to my horror, the boat tipped up with me in it and sank! Luckily the water was only waist deep and I pulled myself, wet through, back onto dry land, cursing my luck. My repairs obviously weren't in the 'Handy Andy' mould.

After an hour or so of more patching up, the boat was ready to go again. Hopefully the leak wouldn't take on too much water during the short time that I was going to be afloat! I was soon to find out as I drifted with a light southerly over the weed bed. Once over the weed an amazing sight met me. Several fish shot off in different directions, with one in particular looking like a pig with fins as it tore off leaving a huge vortex and bow wave. Game on!

I placed three baits in and around the weed with the aid of the chesties and a now badly listing boat. Once again the night passed uneventfully. I gave it until just after dark the following day before resigning myself to another blank. On winding the

baits in I noticed the boilie baits had been whittled away, like an apple core, and the peanut had the skin taken off it. This was particularly odd.

I was going to try and fish the last couple of sessions before the end-of-October finish. With this in mind, I baited the weed bed quite heavily. Odd baits that fell out of the cattie at my feet could clearly be seen almost moving along the lake bed. On further investigation, and with my headtorch almost touching the water, I was shocked to see hundreds of freshwater shrimps covering the dropped baits, literally pushing them around. Once again I left with my tail between my legs. How long would those baits last with a plague of shrimps attacking them? Would the carp struggle to find them covered in shrimps, or could it be like a carp's chocolate éclair?

Pike Action!

The season ground to a halt as October brought with it cold winds and lots of rain, the weed bed seemed to be devoid of life. The only slice of action I had was from pike, on boilies! They took a liking to pop-ups; one of these captures regurgitated several boilies from the evening before. It appeared that if the birds or shrimps didn't wipe me out, then the pike would. The solitude of having the place to myself was good but there was nobody to bounce ideas off or compare results with. I decided to leave the place alone until the end of April. This was the time when the bream started to show and coincided with sightings of carp.

When I returned, I felt that I now had a picture of where I thought the carp would be, thanks to the floating coffin the previous year. The woods seemed devoid of naturals, other than swan mussels, with this bank not receiving much in the way of direct sunlight. The two bays, although weedy, and in what looked to be good conditions, didn't

Steve Broad, looking very different to how he does today, with one of his beloved bream from the northwest stillwater.

see a carp while I was there. Apart from that first encounter in the back pool, I had not seen them feed in there since. The main areas were the ledge and the area in front of the bridge. Both had various depths, weed, proper winds and the sun.

As predicted, the fish started to show from May onwards and this led to a capture! I can, hand on heart, say that I was ecstatic for the captor. If I had to choose who should have caught the first carp, then it would have been Mr Hook – and it was. It was only right that Jeff, who introduced me to the mere, and who had persevered with it himself, even through ill health, should be the one to catch the first carp.

The area, as predicted, was the ledge a little further down from the bridge than I was fishing. I'd watched, a little surprised, as Jeff cast out a broad bean straight out of the tin. This was cast over a couple of small spods of hemp and, a few hours later, it rattled off. I was a little peeved that, due to my rocket-like Primus stove, not only did I not hear the take, I also missed him landing the fish. The first I knew about it, as I tucked into my chilli, was when I looked over in Jeff's direction and saw him frantically waving his hands. Once I made it to his swim, I found him leaning heavily on his car with his inhaler in his hand. The fish had nearly seen him off! Size at the time was irelevent, but for the record it was 25lb 14oz of totally mint common. Surely it'd be my turn soon?

The Swamp

A week later, much to the chagrin of those actually targeting them, I managed a near-12lb, two-tone, classic Cheshire bream, or 'snotty' as we call them. I felt I was getting nearer to catching a carp all the time. On each trip, even if I didn't catch, I had encounters with them. I was getting on the money but, as per usual, time was against me – 24 hours isn't long on these sorts of waters but that's all I had each week.

The end of May gave me some fabulous news; I was accepted into the Mangrove syndicate. I had fished it a few times over the years as a guest, but to get accepted as a member was awesome. The season on there would start on June 12th. This gave me another trip to the mere but then the urge to fish such an exclusive water as the Mangrove would surely be too much to resist, not to mention the outlay in syndicate fees.

So, there was only time for one last chuck of the dice at the mere before the 'swamp', as it is lovingly known, opened. Conditions were textbook – muggy and a southwesterly wind with rain. On arrival I found Steve Broad, fishing for the bream, occupied the bridge swim. I got down a little further than from where Jeff took the broad-bean fish.

"The northwest stillwater was stunning. Set in the grounds of a Gothic castle, it lacked little in atmosphere – truly a fabulous place to fish."

This was the area that I had seen the carp last September. The weed bed was just starting to make some impact, with the chesties being sufficient to drop the baits. Since the pike and the shrimp problem I had stuck with, what is for me, a stunner of a bait on lightly fished waters, peanuts. Used in moderation they don't pose a problem and seem to work best with just a pouchful around the hook bait. Up to this point peanuts had accounted for my PB barbel, chub and now bream (by accident of course!).

I fished the nuts popped-up about six inches. My thinking was that even if the shrimp took the freebies they would not come off the bottom that much. So far this was working, as the baits always came back unwhittled. The night drew a blank, apart from Steve waking me at daft o'clock to take pictures of a bream. We compromised, with him sacking it until daylight. Once light, I wandered the short distance to his swim. The fish was a near Cheshire record at just shy of 14lb. As we rattled the shots off, my remote blasted out a series of bleeps then stopped. I put it down to a bream, so we finished off the photos before I ran back to my swim.

The right-hand rod was forced round to near test curve as it sat clasped between the buzzer and the rod lock. It didn't look like the work of a bream! I quickly slipped the chesties on, steadily winding down to where the line entered the water. The point of entry was only a little further down than where I had placed the bait, but all was solid. Flicking the Baitrunner on, I made my way back. I placed the rod back onto the buzzer while I organised the boat.

Picking the rod back up I eased myself back over where the line entered the water by winding myself to the snag. Once directly over it, I again flicked the Baitrunner on and started to steadily pull the line up. Suddenly the line pinged up, following the direction of the drop-off. Once again I eased my way along, winding ever so slowly, praying that the 15lb Sensor main line and Snake-Bite hooklength would hold out.

I gingerly repeated the process of Baitrnnner on, rod down and steady pressure. I didn't know if whatever I had hooked was still on. There then came some movement; a gentle kick followed by me gaining heavily weeded line. A sight followed this that I will never forget as I saw for the first time what I had hooked – the longest common carp I had ever had the fortune to see. There was no time for the dropped-jaw routine because this magnificent fish surged off, causing me to momentary lose control as my boat span

around in the breeze while I fought to grab the rod.

I cupped the spinning Baitrunner spool in a bid to gain control; this only led to me being pulled along like a whaling boat following a harpooned Moby Dick. I released the spool once again, as this was getting me nowhere quickly, and made my way back to the drop-off where Steve helped me out of the boat. Thankfully, the fish plodded around in open water without snagging again and I managed to regain my composure. Slowly, I started to get the better of the battle with slow pumps of the rod. I feared for the line as, once again, the fish trundled up and down the ledge. Once over this last obstacle, and into the thigh-deep water, Steve expertly scooped up my prize.

As we waded back on to the lawned bank, Jeff arrived right on cue. Once again I thought it quite fitting that he should be involved with the photos and weighing. On the mat the fish was scale perfect, it was probably over a decade since this creature had last graced the bank and this was when they were transferred. Again weight was relatively insignificant but for the record it went 32lb 10oz. My encounter with my own 'undisclosed northwest stillwater' had come to a glorious end.

Cheshire Record

The mere has gone through a number of changes since 1999, when the weed got a stranglehold. This led to a major fish kill wiping out lots of the bream. They followed a northerly wind that also pushed rafts of weed to that end of the mere trapping the bream, which then perished. The knock-on from this was a drop in membership, with more anglers joining to fish solely for the carp. Recently, the mere has seen some of the northwest's most dedicated carp anglers fishing hard on the venue. The mere did the Cheshire record common in 2004, at just over 40lb - a fish that went on to do 43lb in 2005, but sadly died, spawnbound. I am sure this is the fish that looked like a pig with fins bolting from the weed bed back in 1998. The fish I caught went on to do 38lb but sadly, again, it's thought to have since moved on to the great carp lake in the sky.

I am sure that you will agree that fate played a part in my time on this rare beast of a virgin carp lake.

I moved onto the Mangrove a very contented angler, with the knowledge that there wasn't any unfinished business elswere. The start of the season on the Mangrove got off to a flyer for me, taking five fish, including the elusive Cream Fish at 32lb plus. Fate again? Well, that's another story...

Sometimes, just sometimes, the carp gods reward all your effort.

Foreign Fantasy

Frank Warwick's birthday wish comes true when, on a trip to Belgium, his net is graced by a stunning target carp known as The Leopard Fish...

There are so many great memories I have of special occasions where things have really come together to provide events that will remain firmly etched into my mind forever. Yet, for a number of reasons, I have particular fondness and pleasure when I recall the session I am about to relate.

The story starts at a lake of around 80 acres in the north of Belgium. It is a water that I was lucky enough to get on to when I was invited over to take part in the filming of a video in the late 1990s. It is certainly one hell of a water and home to some incredible-looking carp, which are growing at astonishing rates each year. The lake was, and still is, run as a small syndicate by a group of fantastic, like-minded Belgian carpers, with the odd Dutch member, all as keen as mustard and all very special, nice people. I guess you might well have heard of the two blokes who really run the syndicate; they are quite a duo – Johnny and Theo.

This lake is really testament to the sheer hard work and effort that is put in each year by these blokes. It is, in effect, their life's work. They meticulously record captures of each carp, noting details of both weight and length of the fish. Quite often, the length gains of a fish can be just as revealing about a carp's growing potential as the weight is.

They keep a sort of Domesday Book of the fish, with a recent photograph of each side of the fish on record to aid recognition. This book is fascinating and reveals so much information that you can easily get carried away browsing through it, sometimes for hours at a time. A rather nice feature of all this is that if you are lucky enough to capture a previously unknown carp you get to choose its name. Interestingly enough, even after many years, there are still previously uncaught carp popping up very occasionally. On the other hand, there are also some of the lake's character fish, which do get caught a number of times each season. With the meticulous record keeping, you can see which fish slip up more than others and also notice that some carp can go years between captures and basically disappear, almost making everyone think they might have passed away. Then, out of the blue, they get caught and usually show substantial weight gain, showing they are probably more crafty and adept at avoiding rigs or dangerous situations, but are still eating their fair share of the food on offer. Fascinating stuff. In all, I think the lake has around 108 known inhabitants, which is really not a big head of carp for such a decent-sized lake, so each fish is usually hard earned when you catch them!

Off We Go

The session was arranged for mid-October and was set to last for a week. I was going to be accompanied by long-time carp angler Bob Davis, who was eager to sample the special atmosphere of this venue after all I had told him about the place over the previous year.

We were both excited about the prospect of encountering some of the lake's magnificent big commons, which really are something special. I said to Bob: "Just wait until you see the record book, you'll be amazed!" My old friends Johnny and Theo were going to join us and they had both set work aside so we could spend the whole week together. From my previous solitary trip to the lake I had managed to get a rather interesting feel for the place and, perhaps because of my slightly unorthodox approach with single fluoro hook baits, night-time fish finding with the fishfinder and so on, I had been lucky enough to get a stream of captures, including some previously unknown fish which, of course, I got to name!

This provided me with enough tactical matter to really get planning for this new trip. The local lads are in the fortunate position where they can cherry pick the times they fish the lake. They are all keen on prebaiting, which has to be seen to be believed. The sheer quantity of bait they introduce is mind bending. Quite often they will prebait their chosen feature for three weeks, baiting every single day, prior to fishing. No wonder the carp are showing massive weight gains. Can you imagine how

> **"This lake really is a testament to the sheer hard work and effort that is put in each year by these blokes. It is, in effect, their life's work. They meticulously record captures of each carp, noting details of both weight and length of the fish. Quite often the length gains of fish can be just as revealing about a carp's growing potential as weight is."**

My good friends Johnny and Theo – both fantastic blokes and great carp anglers to boot.

confident you would be on the first night's fishing after three weeks of prebaiting, without fishing for them? This is how the Continental lads like to do things. When the prebaiting thing works well, some massive hits can be on the cards.

Ringing The Changes

Bob and I opted to leave nothing to chance, so we covered every bait option and took more than enough quality food bait, which consisted mainly of 18mm and 20mm fishmeals. We chose three different variations so that we could ring the changes and quickly establish a preference, should the carp have one.

Quite importantly in my opinion, there's nothing worse than only taking one bait and finding out the hard way that the carp on a new venue have no enthusiasm for your banker bait and you are stuck with no back-up options!

We took plenty of pellets of various sizes, ranging from 3mm to 20mm maize, hemp, tigers and chopped tigers. I had my usual vast selection of brightly coloured special hook baits in pop-ups and wafters. I also had a good selection of food bait hook baits that were prehardened and fairly breamproof.

From my previous visit to the lake I knew there were very few swims and, as a consequence, we would in all probability be fishing in a line on the main fishing area, where there is a flat section of accessible bank. Most of the bank is steep and very unaccommodating and only fit for solitary fishing. On this trip, though, we were there for both good fishing and a somewhat social occasion, to fish in the company of the guys and renew our friendship after not seeing them for more than a year. With this in mind, I told Bob we needed reels with as big a capacity of line as we could get, so that we could fish distant margins and

I caught this chunky common on my first-ever trip to the lake. We were there to film a DVD/video and we caught our fair share. I loved it there, so I knew I'd be back.

features if necessary. Some of those areas are at more than 400 yards range and with sharp bars and vast weed present, 15lb line was a must, for safety. Bob used the biggest Shimano Baitrunners, the Big Pits; I used my Daiwa Emblem 550s, which also have a very large capacity.

Time To Get Fishing

After a 10-hour journey Bob and I were relieved to finally arrive safely at the venue. Johnny and Theo were there to meet us and start our session and, as I suspected, we were all going to fish in a line together on the long social bank.

Johnny and Theo fished on the left-hand side so they could cover their favourite area, a prominent plateau at around 75 yards. This had been the scene of many of their magnificent captures and was their favourite area to prebait. I let Bob choose his swim next, especially as it was his first visit! I ended up on the far right-hand side, which suited me just fine, as I always prefer to be on the end when fishing in a line – very important indeed.

The Belgian lads have some fantastic boats permanently moored at the lake, some of which are solid metal – very stable they are too! They thoughtfully let us use some of their electric motors and batteries, making life easier. Bob and I went out together and I showed him one of the seldom-fished lakes, with very interesting features. Basically, it has a very narrow, long bar that runs the entire length of the lake at about 320 yards range, and tapers gradually away from you until it's more than 500 yards plus and well out of range of even the biggest-capacity reels. Bob agreed this feature looked highly attractive and needed to be explored fully. While out there we took the opportunity to carefully mark, with H-block markers, any tasty-looking features

A single hook bait cast at showing fish resulted in this lovely mirror on my very first trip. I was well and truly hooked and really loved being on the venue with my friends.

This carp, which I nicknamed The Moose, had never been caught before. We'd have known if it had, as the records they keep over their are meticulous to say the least.

and designating swim boundaries.

The weather was excellent, warm westerlies blowing with intermittent cloud and sunny spells. On impulse, I prepared a couple of Sensas groundbait buckets full of a mixture of various boilies, hemp, maize, tigers and lots of sizes of pellets. I decided to use one of my favourite additions to any bait for carp fishing, tuna-fish oil. I have mentioned it many times before and I am 100 per cent confident in the tuna's powers of attraction. The type I use is the sort you get containing sunflower oil. This is amazing stuff, no doubt about that! I hastily opened four tins of the stuff and poured the fishy-smelling oil all over the mixed buckets of bait, liberally glugging them and mixing the potent concoction together. Bob used his mix without the tuna-oil addition. I wanted to check out the difference on this water, to see if the same profound effect was in evidence as on other waters I had tried it on.

The slick from the oil on my baits looked superb when I baited up and lasted a good number of hours. I placed each hook bait carefully in turn, taking the rod out with me on each occasion. I was very particular with rig and bait placement, raising the rig up and down on the top of the featured bar I wanted to fish. Amazingly, the echo sounder showed a dotted line bouncing up off the bottom each time I raised and lowered the rig, leaving a clear trace, showing me I was exactly on top of the very narrow bar, which was only three or four feet wide on the ridge. This was the difference between fishing 16 feet on top or 24 feet if you missed it and dropped down the bar's slope!

Make Or Break

Sometimes it would take several attempts to drop the rig in perfect position. It is of the utmost importance, and when you think of those long, inactive periods sat behind rods, it is well worth spending extra time on important details that can make or break your trip.

I used double baits on the rigs snowman style, to avoid the lake's many bream, with a 20mm fishmeal bottom bait underneath and an 18mm or 16mm hi-viz pop-up on top to balance the presentation. Hooks were size 6 or 8 long shanks, usually used with a clear shrink-tube line aligner and shrink-tube blow-back set-up. I also used 5oz or 6oz leads, usually Korda flatliners, on a safety-clip set-up. For extra security and fish safety I attached the leads via a weak length of 4lb nylon.

"The slick from the oil on my baits looked superb when I baited up and lasted a good number of hours. I placed each hook bait carefully in turn, taking the rod with me."

Conditions looked very good and I had a really good feeling about this session. I just hoped the carp agreed with me!

Despite fishing at a really big distance, my first take, when it came, gave us warning via a bleep or two, it just went into meltdown and gave that satisfying solid irresistible pressure as I set the hook. To avoid complications I opted to take to the boat and shorten the distance between the carp and I as quickly as possible, mostly due to my need to avoid fish burying themselves in the severe Canadian pondweed beds. On this occasion, my rig ejected the lead. This made one hell of a difference and soon a hefty, big mirror broke the surface; I guessed it was an upper thirty. My estimate proved to be accurate, as the scales read 37lb 11oz. What a nice start. I suspected that this was a sign of things to come, as my plan started to come together.

Mad Timepieces

Although warm in the day, the nights were drawing in and it would chill rapidly as soon as the sun dropped below the horizon. The peace of the lake would be intermittently broken by the various chimes or peal of bells from the many churches that abound in adjacent villages. If you awoke in the middle of the night you would always be aware of the time due to these mad timepieces.

After repositioning the rod and pinpointing the ridge, I was extremely confident of more action. A while later I received a single bleep and scrambled over to the rods to see if it was a drop back developing. The same rod gave a second bleep on the indicator and my quiver-arm indicator visibly twitched back, signalling something was occurring! Without further ado, I wound down for what seemed ages and made contact with some resistance. "Oh no, not a bloody bream," I commented to Bob. Then the resistance suddenly escalated and I knew it was a carp. As previously, I took to the boat and pumped the carp in, trying to keep constant pressure on the fish as the electric outboard sped me to my unseen prize. When fishing such extreme distance you don't always know how big the carp is, as the stretch in your main line, if you are using nylon, acts as a big shock absorber and diffuses the power of the fish. The power of what I was connected to was absorbed by this effect until I got to within about 30 yards of my target, when the rod was violently wrenched over as a ridiculously long common broke surface and manically exploded, thrashing the water to a foam. Once in the net, the common turned out to be the longest carp I had ever seen, at well over one metre long. It was long and lean however, without any gut, but it still slammed the scales round to just under 36lb!

Things were going well for me, but Bob had yet to get off the mark. I have to admit it crossed my mind more than once that my inclusion of the tuna-fish oil could be making that vital difference and, despite Bob being quite close to me, the carp were perhaps being enticed my way? At least that was what I was suspecting!

A Happy Man

With five more days and nights ahead I was a very happy man, and my mind kept wandering back to the record book. As I had browsed through this book, a few outrageously magnificent-looking creatures had caught my eye. I remarked that, despite it not being the biggest common in the lake, I would, if given the choice, love to catch an awesome creature aptly named The Leopard. Even better would be if I could catch the beauty on my impending birthday! To me, at that moment, I wanted that particular carp more than any other in the world. Little did I know, but fate was going to arrange a meeting between us sooner than I could ever have imagined.

The following day, after an uneventful night, I noticed on the echo sounder, while out rebaiting and repositioning my rods, that fish were in evidence at the very extreme distant part of the underwater ridge that tapered away from my swim. This meant that I might not have enough line on the reels to get baits to the new spots. Bugger it, I had to try! I dropped my rig carefully on the adjacent area. Then, being very careful not to get any belly in the line, and also avoiding dislodging my lead and rig, I shot back to the bank. I knew it was going to be a close-run thing and alarmingly my spool was emptying at a rapid rate of knots. In fact, well before I hit the bank, I could see the metal base of the spool on my reel. As I reached the bank there was less than four turns of line on the reel - that was how close it was. And so it went with each of my other three rods, with one spool actually emptying before I hit the bank. On that rod I got a spool of 12lb line and put 20 yards on the base of the spool and attached all the paid-out line by way of a shockleader knot! I had no choice! I locked up all the rods solid with butt rings behind the buzzers and sat at the rods, alert and ready to take to the boat immediately should a take occur. I hoped the stretch in the line would give me some margin for error. God knows what the outcome would have been should a powerful, screaming run occur like the first fish had given me!

"After signalling a few bleeps, my indicator sprang tight and I hit the take in an instant and literally flew into the boat, winding like a madman, trying to regain some line."

Something told me what I was doing was going to yield the reward. I felt I was fishing an area that, in all probability, had never seen a hook bait, almost a sanctuary area due to the distance problem. The answer was not slow in coming. After signalling a few bleeps, my indicator sprang tight and I hit the take in an instant and literally flew into the boat, winding like a madman, frantically trying to regain some line on my near-empty spool. Yet again my drop off lead worked like a dream and I could enjoy a tremendous armaching battle out over my distant hotspot. A deep-bodied, mint-condition mirror surfaced from the murky depths and its flanks showed heavy red and pink colouration, no doubt from the Robin Red content of its diet, which all the lads bang in the lake all summer long. Yet another mid-thirty and pleasing, although I wondered if I would latch into one of the lake's very big fish soon? If the law of averages was anything to go by, a big one would surely come!

Another Take

A pattern was emerging and hot times for feeding became apparent. I was getting two or three takes a day and never got two takes from the exact same spot. It was almost like the carp avoided the localised area of capture once it had occurred, but replacing the rig and lightly baiting a new spot would throw up another take.

I was happy, but also feeling for Bob, as he had yet to have a take despite being virtually on top of me. The rigs and bait were very similar; the only difference was the oil and glug. It quite simply had to be a

One of two 38lb mirrors, caught just 15 minutes apart. Look at the size of the pectoral fins on it – a truly impressive carp.

Long-time carp angler Bob Davis with a whacking-great common from the Belgian lake. What a result!

The angry common, at 44lb 6oz. The commons we caught were magnificent, but the one I was after still eluded me.

I enjoyed my birthday while out at the Belgian lake. The boys even provided the finest Belgian-chocolate cake.

An absolute cracker, and a new lake record mirror at 47lb 7oz. This place was amazing.

strong factor. Bob decided a change of swim was called for, so he moved on a fresh wind to the far end of the lake. I hoped it would pay off and I reluctantly agreed he had very little option, as time was now running short.

Happy Birthday

I woke up on October 23rd, another year older, and was a bit embarrassed to see Johnny and Theo had been busy and there, outside my bivvy, was a rather large chocolate birthday cake with loads of candles on it, bringing home to me just how bloody old I was getting! A very thoughtful, great gesture from the lads, though. Just as I was losing my moustache and eyebrows from the heat of the candles on the cake as I went to blow them out, I had a very obvious violent take. With no time to spare, I played the carp hard from the bank and knew from the feel that I was playing a big fish. Unfortunately, this fish found a weed bed, so I had to get above it in the boat. After quite a few anxious moments, a giant ball of Canadian weed surfaced with a mind-blowing common charging around like a mad bull beneath it. Theo, who had accompanied me in the boat, raised his eyebrows and said in a matter of fact way: "Frank, you are playing The Leopard." With that I concentrated as though my life depended on it.

Eventually, after a heart-stopping time, when I had to slacken off while Theo got rid of a massive ball of weed from my main line, the aptly named Goliath named The Leopard was mine.

She was not quite 40lb, but did I care? Did I buggery. It was the sheer look of that creature that made pounds and ounces irrelevant. One of my favourite carp of all time.

That night I caught a big angry common more than 5lb bigger. I was ecstatic, but The Leopard was the one for me, that was for sure. Bob came good on the very last morning and his move paid off. He slipped the net under his new personal-best common of 46lb 4oz and had a 28lb mirror to crown what had been a very special session.

I have been back a couple of times to that very special lake and it has been very kind to me. Indeed, a year later, I was lucky enough to have a lake record mirror of 47lb 7oz.

So, to Johnny, Theo and all the boys, thanks for the memories. I have really enjoyed recounting them here and it's almost been like reliving them all over again.

I hope you, the readers, enjoy them as much as I did.

My favourite common of all time, and one that I caught in uncanny circumstances – The Leopard.

The Centurion

The inimitable Derek Ritchie tells of an awesome haul of 100 carp over 20lb in just one season...

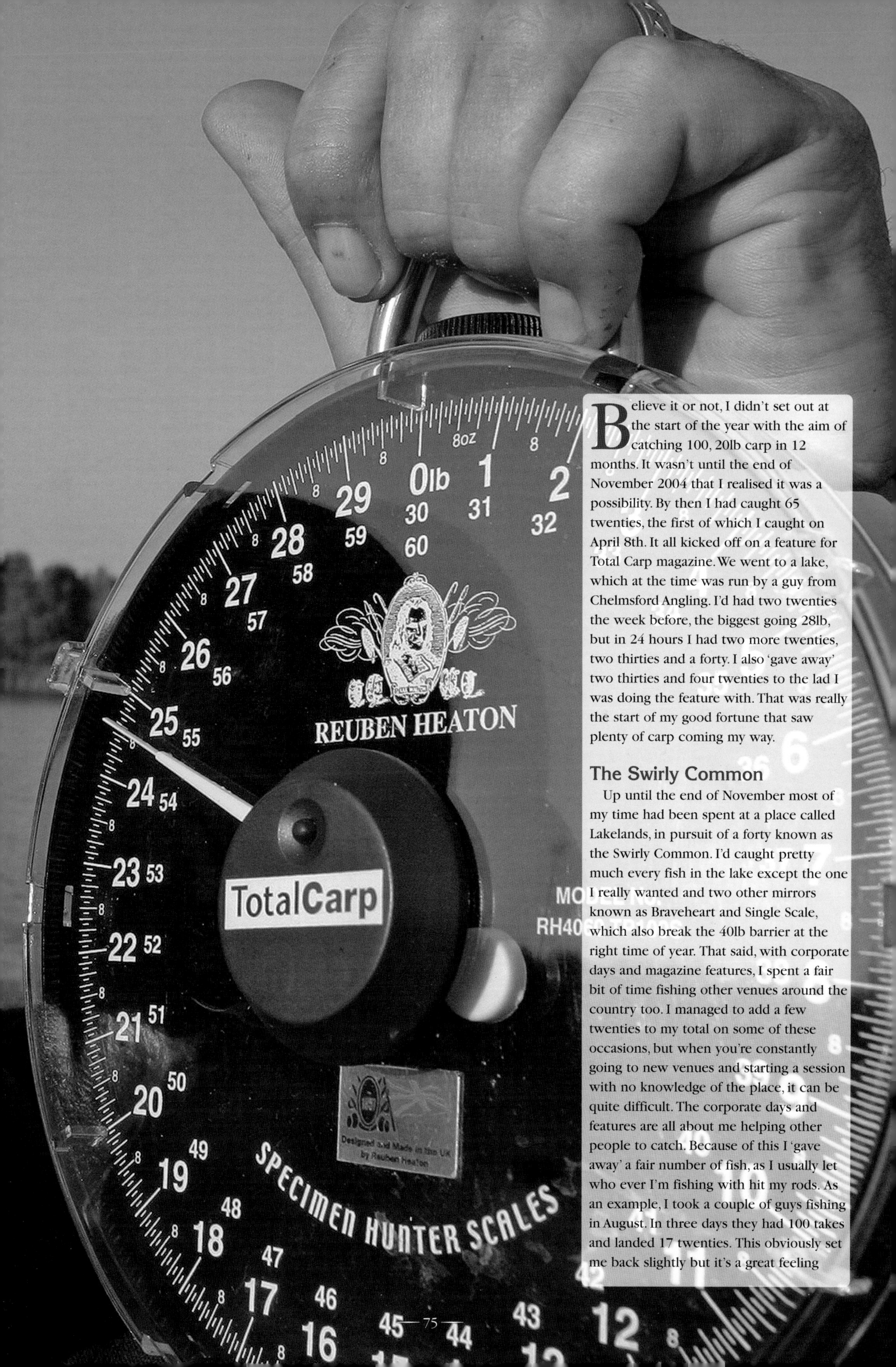

Believe it or not, I didn't set out at the start of the year with the aim of catching 100, 20lb carp in 12 months. It wasn't until the end of November 2004 that I realised it was a possibility. By then I had caught 65 twenties, the first of which I caught on April 8th. It all kicked off on a feature for Total Carp magazine. We went to a lake, which at the time was run by a guy from Chelmsford Angling. I'd had two twenties the week before, the biggest going 28lb, but in 24 hours I had two more twenties, two thirties and a forty. I also 'gave away' two thirties and four twenties to the lad I was doing the feature with. That was really the start of my good fortune that saw plenty of carp coming my way.

The Swirly Common

Up until the end of November most of my time had been spent at a place called Lakelands, in pursuit of a forty known as the Swirly Common. I'd caught pretty much every fish in the lake except the one I really wanted and two other mirrors known as Braveheart and Single Scale, which also break the 40lb barrier at the right time of year. That said, with corporate days and magazine features, I spent a fair bit of time fishing other venues around the country too. I managed to add a few twenties to my total on some of these occasions, but when you're constantly going to new venues and starting a session with no knowledge of the place, it can be quite difficult. The corporate days and features are all about me helping other people to catch. Because of this I 'gave away' a fair number of fish, as I usually let who ever I'm fishing with hit my rods. As an example, I took a couple of guys fishing in August. In three days they had 100 takes and landed 17 twenties. This obviously set me back slightly but it's a great feeling when you help someone else catch a big carp, the looks on their faces is priceless.

Well, by the end of November it was time for a change of venue. Lakelands pretty much shuts up shop through winter, so I didn't see the point in wasting my time in a stubborn attempt to catch the Swirly Common. The plan was to return the following spring and resume my quest. So I was left looking for a venue to fish throughout winter.

Aveley Lake

About 20 minutes from my house is a place known as Aveley Lake. It's about 25 acres and reaches depths of 48 feet in places. The stock in this lake is quite incredible, with about 18 to 20 thirties and a huge head of twenties. It's a great winter water, which is why I chose to target it. It was at this point I realised catching 100, 20lb carp by the start of April 2005 was a possibility. But, and it was a big but, I had the hardest months ahead of me and I still had 35 twenties to catch.

With my new job at Svendsen Sports I had to move from using the Mainline Fusion to one of the DD Bait boilies. I phoned Mads Grossell in Denmark, the bait guru responsible for DD Bait, and had a lengthy conversation with him about which baits to use throughout winter. I explained what I was trying to achieve and that I was on a bit of a deadline with that side of things, so I needed a productive winter season.

"Don't worry Derek, I have just the thing," said Mads in a rather confident tone before putting the phone down.

Two days later, 50kg of Kiwi Crustacean boilies, a pallet of tinned mussels and a sack of krill powder turned up on my doorstep. Mads wasn't lying, he did have just the thing, and this was it.

Done By Christmas

During the first week on Aveley I had 20 takes, 11 of which resulted in twenties. That took my total to 76. I thought to myself: "I'll have done it by Christmas." But it never happened.

All the takes at Aveley come during the night, so even if I was busy in the day I could still grab an overnighter here and there so I still had a chance of catching.

In fact, there was a point in January when I didn't think I was going to do it. The fish moved from the area I was catching them in and I had to go and find them again. I had just set up in the swim I'd been concentrating on and I saw a fish jump on the opposite side of the lake, tight against the reeds in The Snag swim. I packed everything down and like a grasshopper, which is what they call me on Aveley, I moved. Luckily the move paid off and I started catching almost immediately.

For the first half of the year I didn't spend a great deal of time on the bank, not as much as people seem to think anyway. At that time I was working five days a week at Brentwood Angling and could only get two nights and one day fishing a week. In August everything changed. I signed up for Svendsen Sports and suddenly I was able to spend four days a week out on the bank. It goes without saying that the extra fishing time was a massive help and it was at this point when I really started adding to my total. In the first two weeks of working for Svendsen Sports I had seven twenties and four thirties, although anything weighing 30lb and above wasn't added to the tally. I had planned to put in a lot of time during winter because I do less corporate days and get more time to myself. As it turned out, with shows, holidays and other commitments, I didn't put in as much time as I would have liked. In fact, there was a three-week period around Christmas when I didn't get to go fishing at all. The saving grace was that all the takes at Aveley come during the night, so even if I was busy in the day I could still grab an overnighter here and there and stand a good chance of catching. So, throughout the colder months, as most of you were sitting down to eat your dinner, I was out there hauling.

I must admit that I did use a fair bit of bait over the 12-month period and I'm sure this was key to my success. During summer on Lakelands I was using up to 30kg of bait a session. One of the problems I encountered on there was the 'chickens', or coots as they're better known. They would wipe out a bed of boilies in no time, and having chickens continually diving on your baits doesn't do a great deal for your fishing. I started substituting the boilies for pellets, particles and sweetcorn, which the birds seemed to ignore. I was still using boilies, but nowhere near as many as I started off with.

Winter On Aveley

Through the winter months on Aveley I cut the amount of bait right down. During my four days I would typically use 7kg of boilies, as well as the mussels and krill powder, which I mixed together to form a groundbait. The plan to keep the carp coming throughout winter was simple. I would find an area of the lake where the

#23 This mid-twenty was caught in the early hours of the morning. It fell for a small 'stick' and 14mm boilie hook bait. What a stunner.

#30 This scraper twenty from Lakelands came along while I was targeting the big common. It helped up my total, so it was more than welcome.

#41 At 23lb this is a perfect example of the typical strain of carp in Aveley Lake. There are loads of these in there making it a great winter water.

carp seemed to shoal up and keep the bait going into that area. The carp should eventually accept my boilies as an easy supply of quality food and readily eat them. I selected a swim I nicknamed The Burning Bush, as it had a bush jutting out at 60 yards from a reed bed that ran the entire width of the lake. Using a marker rod I found an area of clay chips, which are the main features in Aveley, at 90 yards and started my baiting campaign. I made sure that 7kg of Kiwi Crustacean boilies went onto this spot every week, to get the carp into a routine of visiting here to feed. I was using a boilie rocket to get the baits out there. If you've ever used one you'll know that they don't hold many baits. In fact, the one I had took eight 14mm baits at a time. It would take anything up to two hours to get all the bait out. I think most people would have thrown the rod down and gone home, it certainly crossed my mind a few times, but I just kept on going. After a few weeks I started baiting a patch of clay chips just off the bush in the reed bed. As it was closer than the original spot I could control the baiting a bit more and even fire a few balls of the mussel and krill mix out there too. Unfortunately, the carp weren't the only ones who discovered my constant bait supply. After a month or two the curse of the chickens caught up with me once more and the coots were constantly wiping out my baited areas. It got to a point where a mass of birds would descend on my swim as soon as I picked up the spod rod. The only way around it was to bait up at night. This wasn't ideal because most of the bites come during the night and I don't like spodding on top of feeding fish, but it had to be done. It was obviously working, as every carp I landed started crapping my bait out on the unhooking mat; so they were on it. Seeing that gave me a massive confidence boost too, I was obviously doing something right.

The Key To Success

There's no doubt in my mind that keeping the bait going in regularly was the key to my success. Because I had a period of a few weeks around Christmas where I couldn't get to the lake, the carp's regular bait supply dried up. Even though people were fishing in my swim on the spots that I'd been baiting, very few carp were caught. The key difference between my approach and theirs was the amount of bait. Whereas I was firing in a regular supply of boilies, the other anglers stuck to PVA bags and single baits.

> **"I endured some pretty horrendous weather, I think it got down to -8°C at the coldest point, but I would do it all over again to get that sense of achievement."**

As soon as I returned and started baiting again, the carp came back. I had three carp on my first session after Christmas but then, for some reason, the bulk of the fish decided to move to The Snag swim on the opposite bank.

Because I was catching so much more than most of the anglers on Aveley I had people coming into my swim to check out what I was doing. Quite a few of them were under the impression that I had a new wonder rig that was slaying all the carp, but they couldn't have been further from the truth. Most of the anglers asked me what I was doing and when I told them they couldn't believe how simple my approach was. However, there were one or two anglers who, I think, were too proud to ask me what I was doing. Instead, they hung around the swim trying to get a sneaky look at the rigs and baits I was using. I couldn't resist a chance to wind them up. When they wandered into my swim I would pretend to hide bits of tackle, as if I had something I really didn't want them to see. It drove them crazy and they spent ages trying to catch a glimse of my 'wonder rigs'. All they had to do was ask and they could have saved themselves a lot of time! Truth is, my rigs were probably the same as theirs anyway.

The carp were feeding on my bait so confidently that I don't think the rig made a lot of difference. When it becomes a 'riggy' water I reckon it's because the fish are scared of picking up the baits. They don't suck them into their mouths confidently; they constantly pick them up and drop them. Continual baiting goes a long way to

'Fly my beauties, fly!' I applied bait steadily throughout the year, and have no doubts that getting the carp to accept my bait as a valuable food source was the key to the constant success on Aveley.

#54 A quick change of swim resulted in this 24lb 4oz mirror from the Sheep Bank at Aveley Lake. A steady baiting campaign was key to my success.

#87 After struggling to catch for a couple of days, this 28lb 8oz mirror came as a huge relief. Persistence really did pay off in this instance.

After catching the 100 twenties I went back to Lakelands for my target fish, the Swirly Common. Here she is, all 41lb of her. What a beauty!

> **"By march it had all changed. I'd got my total number up to 90 and when you're that close to reaching your goal your whole mindset changes. I started to worry about not making 100."**

eliminating this. All of my fish, except a couple in summer, came to a simple bottom-bait approach. I had a 7in coated-braid hooklength, with a size 8 ProLogic C2, long-shanked hook and I added a little stick, made from the mussel and krill mix, onto the hooklength. It doesn't get much simpler than that.

Speed Fishing

In essence I was speed fishing, catching as many carp as I could in my allotted time. This is when I discovered the beauty of quick-change clips. All of my hooklengths were attached via these and I would have at least six spare hooklengths baited and ready to go.

Each time I landed a fish, I unclipped the hooklength, attached a new one, and I was fishing again within seconds. There were definitely distinct bite times during winter and it was important to cash in when the fish were feeding. I remember a couple of times when I'd recast, dealt with the fish I had just landed and, as I was returning it, the rod roared off again. It was so important not to waste any time with rods out of the water, so preparation was a key part of my approach.

Back On 'Em

After I'd moved and found the fish again I slowly started to add to my total once more. It was a strange feeling really because, up until that point, I wasn't overly fussed about reaching my target. Obviously I thought it'd be nice to achieve it but I wouldn't lose any sleep if I didn't. By March all that had changed. I'd got my total number of twenties up to 90 and when you're that close to reaching your goal your whole mindset changes. I started to worry about not reaching the magical 100 mark.

I was now determined to catch another 10 twenties, even if it meant spending every conceivable minute at the lakeside. I didn't care if it was pouring with rain, freezing cold or snowing. A hurricane could have hit Essex and I would have still gone fishing.

March was a slow month and, with

Night-time is bite time on Aveley so I had to endure a lot of rod watching. Single bleeps in the winter could often mean carp on!

Making Del's 'Ton-Up' Stick Mix

STEP ONE
A tin of Real Mussell Meat is the first ingredient to go into Del's mix concoction.

STEP TWO
Next into the mix go a couple of handfuls of DD Bait Elips pellets.

STEP THREE
The mussels and the pellets are then mixed together thoroughly in a bucket.

STEP FOUR
Next, Del adds a generous amount of krill powder, which he rates highly.

STEP FIVE
The mix is then 'wetted' with 20 to 30ml of DD Bait Insect Juice – mmmm, nice!

STEP SIX
Another thorough mixing and it's job done, Del's ultra-effective stick mix is ready to go!

getting roped into doing a few shows, I'd missed out on a few crucial days' fishing. With just four days to go my tally was stuck at 96. Talk about going down to the wire! I arrived at the lake on a Monday morning, knowing that I had to catch four twenties before Friday. Typically, the weather was awful, with clear skies and freezing temperatures conspiring against me, but that always seems to be the way when you're up against it. I'm sure you've had times when everything tries to stop you from achieving your goal. Anyway, I set up, went through the motions and sat there hopeful, but not too confident - what else could I do?

Imagine my surprise when a run in the early hours of the morning had me standing on the water's edge, in freezing temperatures, wearing just a pair of tracksuit bottoms, a T-shirt and a pair of socks, playing a fish. When I finally landed the fish and hoisted it onto the scales, the needle settled on 24lb. Suddenly, being cold, and now rather wet, didn't matter. One down, three to go. By daybreak I had managed to catch another, a heavily plated mirror of 22lb.

With two captures under my belt on the first night I was feeling rather confident, a massive difference from 24 hours previous. The Tuesday passed without event, but that's not unusual at Aveley, as the hours of darkness are when the fish feed. That night was almost a repeat performance of the first, with twenties number 99 and, finally, 100, falling foul of the Kiwi Crustacean boilies. As soon as I saw number 100 break the surface I knew it was a good twenty.

At that point my heart was in my mouth and I really didn't want to be playing it, I just wanted it to swim into the net and for it all to be over. I can't describe the feeling as that final fish slipped over the net cord. I had such a sense of achievement, relief and a slight smug feeling as well.

I sacked the fish in the deep margins and as soon as it got light, just two hours later, I phoned a few of my mates to come and take some photos. As I was so close to the mark before the session I had bought a couple of celebratory bottles of Champagne, just in case I caught the 100th twenty. I didn't want to jinx myself, but by the same token I felt an achievement like this needed to be celebrated in style. After the photos I popped the corks and toasted the carp gods.

Achieving Your Goals

It's always nice to set yourself goals and have something to aim for but, at the end of the day, I just enjoy going fishing. It doesn't matter how big the fish are as long as you're doing something you want to do and really enjoying yourself. After all, that's what carp fishing is all about, enjoying yourself.

The thought of achieving the goal you've set makes you try much harder. If you've put the time and effort into whatever it is you're aiming for, that final moment makes all the effort worthwhile.

Through the winter I endured some pretty horrendous weather, I think it got down to minus 8°C at the coldest point, but I would do it all over again to get that sense of achievement.

The best advice I can give to someone who wants to do something similar is to keep going. You have to be regimented in your approach and almost force yourself to tie that spare rig, spend hours baiting up, or get out of bed in the middle of the night to recast. It is a lot of effort but believe me, it's worth it. It's much easier, I know, to not bother, but then you never realise your goals and ambitions. You have to make the effort at all times.

Once I'd caught the 100th twenty I set my sights on a new target, the British record, the famous Two Tone in Conningbrook. Now, didn't a certain Mr Levy say he was going there too?

"As soon as it got light I phoned a few friends to come and take the photos. I'd brought a few bottles of Champagne for this trip, just in case I caught my 100th twenty. I felt an achievement like this needed to be celabrated in style so, once the photos were all done, I popped a few corks and toasted the carp gods!"

Dave Lane takes camou to the extreme in a bid to blend in at Sonning Eye.

Heartbreak, Hard Work And Salvation

Adam Penning's skill, effort and determination abound in this tale of one of his finest captures to date...

It was 1999 and most of my fishing was spent on Linear Manor in pursuit of the famous Popeye and Cut Tail. The campaign was productive and I managed 27 captures; this being before the 'aliens' were introduced. Cut Tail eluded me right to the end and when I eventually hooked her on a floater at the beginning of September, she came adrift just off the net cord after a dramatic 10-minute scrap. Fish losses go with the territory; to some extent you learn how to cope with them but inevitably some really affect you. This was one of those heart-wrenching losses because I'd spent a lot of time and effort in pursuit of that carp.

Ultimately, Cut Tail and Popeye eluded me and I had to endure the experience of finding the corpse of the latter and then burying her earlier that spring. During the campaign I had caught just about every other fish in the lake and I knew in my heart of hearts that there was no way I was going to wade back through them all again just to get to Cut Tail. It was over, a bitter end to a great experience and it was time to move on.

The New Challenge

I was eager for a new challenge and hungry for a shot at my first forty, but where should I go? There are plenty of waters that hold carp in excess of 40lb but, for an angler fishing weekends only, many are simply an impractical option.

Through my friend Martin Bowler, my attention had been drawn to Elstow Pit Two. Although the water was classed as more than a bit challenging, it was quiet and seemed to be the perfect place to continue my search for a forty. Pit Two was then around 25 acres, although flooding in recent years has somewhat extended an area of shallows. Being an old clay pit, like many others in that area, it had sheer banks and very deep expanses of water.

The stock of carp was around 18 fish, but two of these could be discounted as practical targets as The Mother and Speckles hadn't been caught for almost five years. Although The Mother was the first of the fish to break through the 40lb barrier, the known big one that did get regularly caught was a carp called The Twin and this often topped the 40lb mark. The rest of the stock consisted of some corking old mirrors, many of which were very rarely caught.

The third largest in the lake was a mirror known as Lisa. This fish had been up to almost 40lb in the past and was a real old warrior. Scaley was another one that I dearly wanted to catch; a stunning, very heavily plated mirror of 33 to 34lb and another that was very rarely caught. The next member of the 'A Team' was Epaulettes, so named because of its large plated shoulder scales, which are reminiscent of military rank. This fish was a mid-thirty, similar looking to The Twin and one that only came out once or twice each season.

The last of the known big ones was Speckles. Her last capture had seen her weighing just under 30lb.

For those unfamiliar, Pit Two is a very inhospitable clay pit that has some extremely deep water. The deepest I found was 32 feet, which both tactically and psychologically takes some dealing with. The banks are generally very steep; so steep in fact that they are perfect for pushing old cars off, and one of the first things you see

when you walk onto one corner of the lake are two rusty, wrecked hatchbacks at the bottom of 25 feet of water! The banks were covered in thick bramble bushes and there aren't any swims as such. Coupled with this, the lake is adjacent to a landfill site and gets plagued with horseflies. I guess that all helped to keep the place so quiet!

One On The Bank

The first journey there took just over three hours and I arrived to an unexpectedly busy lake, just on darkness. Due to some incredibly warm March weather, with strong sunshine and temperatures up to 16°C, I opted to set up at the entrance to a shallow reedy bay. I was hoping to intercept any carp that may be travelling onto the shallows to take advantage of the unseasonably warm weather. This first session was only a recce and all I was hoping for was to see a fish, and to begin to get a feel for the place.

There were four other anglers on the lake and from afar I could see that one of them was into a fish a little before 9am. Winding in, I wandered around, hoping that I would be lucky enough to see one of these special fish on my very first visit. The swim in question was The Carpet; this was on the opposite side of the lake and it took me quite some time to make my way there. By the time I arrived the fish was lying on the mat, and what an incredible-looking beast it was. I was informed that it was Epaulettes and she looked immaculate and solid in her late-winter colours. A weight of 34lb 10oz was recorded and I felt privileged to help out with the photos of such a wonderful-looking old carp.

To say I packed up on a high would be an understatement. The capture gave me great confidence that the carp were indeed catchable from such depths, but also trashed my theory that they would quickly move into warmer, shallow water in such high-pressure conditions - the captor had found success with a single hook bait in 28 feet of water!

Stitched Up

The spring period was unusually busy for the pit and some Friday nights I would turn up and find a dozen other anglers. When you bear in mind that the lake can be easily stitched up by less than half that amount, it was very frustrating. Often, I simply had to take whatever was left over and just fill in a gap somewhere. I knew it wasn't great angling, but what else could I do?

I did however make a few chances and managed to get on a big mirror that was feeding in the Diving Boards area one Sunday afternoon. On this occasion the clock beat me and although everything looked perfect for a take, I had to pack up a few hours later.

The only angler to consistently score during that spring was Phil Da Silva. Phil was self employed and shifted his work so

"To say I packed up on a high would be an understatement. The capture gave me great confidence that the carp were indeed catchable from such depths."

With the wind rippling in it looked perfect and before long I had two slack lines hanging from the rod tips, pointing vaguely towards the precise margin traps I had set.

that he could always be at the lake when it mattered. I spent a lot of pleasant hours in his company and he was an invaluable phone contact - always giving me the latest when I called during the weekdays. It was perhaps inevitable that an angler of Phil's calibre would score heavily and his first take was Lisa at 35lb 8oz, in the first week of April. This was the second carp of the year and was caught from a swim that is very close to a shallow, snaggy area. Spring was very much in the air and I felt that, with the weather constantly improving, this would be the area the next bite would come from.

With that came the snow! It was April 12th and I sat at home looking out at the white-coated cars, hardly believing my eyes! The subsequent session was, not surprisingly, a bitterly cold blank but the weather slowly got better towards the Easter weekend. This is one of my favourite times of the year because I get to fish a whole four-night session without sacrificing any of my then-meagre holiday entitlement.

As expected, the lake was packed out and, as Phil occupied my first swim choice, I decided to follow my previous hunch and fish the snags in front of the steep cliff area.

Although it was far from warm, I suspected one or two might drift in - after all I had four whole nights at my disposal. As it happened, I blanked again but Phil triumphed, taking a further three fish over the course of a week-long session: Lisa at 34lb 8oz, Little Shoulders at 23lb 12oz and The Midget at 19lb 9oz. All the bites came from the Slope swim, which covered the entrance to the only other area of shallow water.

At this point I had fished a lot of rod hours but found the going, in terms of other angler pressure, very tricky indeed. This year was turning out to be the busiest ever on the lake and I just couldn't fish where I wanted, when I wanted and felt that I would catch if only I could fish on my own terms. That, however, just wasn't going to be possible and with things set to get even busier, I decided to pull off and wait for things to quieten down. Phil deservedly caught The Twin in early May at 43lb, but by then I was long gone...

Unknown Whackers

After a couple of months spent chasing unknown whackers in the Cotswolds, I returned for a weekend session in the second week of July. As I had expected, the lake was practically deserted - there was only one other angler! Now I could fish properly and I really was buzzing as I walked around the pit looking for the fish. Eventually, in the sweltering afternoon sunshine, I found a few lying up in a weed bed close to the main snags. Some big, grey scaly backs were visible and, with a real sense of purpose and expectation, I set up pitch in the snags corner.

With the wind gently rippling in it looked perfect and before long I had two slack lines hanging from the rod tips, pointing vaguely towards the very precise marginal traps I had set. With the light indicators laying in the water it looked good, very good, and for the first time I really felt in the zone. However, the night passed without event, as did the following morning, even though the fish were clearly still in the area. The temperatures continued to rise and I sat back behind my camou screen and waited.

By mid-afternoon it became incredibly hot and humid. The wind had totally disappeared and the odd fish I could see was lying completely still in the thick weed. I had tried firing floaters out at various points since my arrival but, as is usual for Pit Two, the carp totally ignored them.

Then, early evening, the change came. Without warning and with great speed, thick grey clouds loomed in the southwest, racing towards me on a strengthening wind. Instantly, the carp disappeared from view, but I thought I had a pretty good idea where they'd be heading.

I ran around the main headlands and arrived breathlessly in the Slope area. This was the area that the wind was beginning to slam into with force. This was too good a chance to miss and after a while I had moved all my gear. The torrent of sweat pouring down my face was being quickly dried by the fresh wind but the move had been a proper backbreaker without my faithful carp barrow. This had become a casualty and was stashed in the car after suffering its fourth puncture since the start of my campaign.

Before dark I managed to get three rods well positioned in quite 'normal' depths of water. The best thing was that I seemed to have arrived before the carp and I'd had time to carefully set all my traps in preparation. Now I was angling!

I fished the base of the marginal shelf with two rods, carefully plumbing it to find the exact point where the shelf finished and the bottom levelled out. It was smooth, clean and 11 feet deep. The third rod was cast to a small clay and gravel hump to my left which also looked prime - it was right in the centre of the channel leading to a bay, which was also receiving the force of the wind.

All three rods had stiff rigs with fishmeal pop-ups that I had hand-rolled and glugged in salmon oil. A few boilies and a few pouches full of Hinders Elips pellets completed each trap and, as the waves began to splash into the buzzer bars, I opened a bottle of rioja and dug myself in under the brolly. Due to the flooded and marshy nature of the swim, I'd waded my rods right out into the water to gain better line angles.

Sleepless Night

The night was very turbulent and very carpy - I found sleep impossible to come by. The wind was so strong that I had to get up in the middle of the night and turn the brolly around. Although the wind and rain made hearing any sound from the lake an impossibility, I could imagine great big carp launching themselves out among the waves; it was one of those nights when you felt it could go off at any moment.

Due to the lack of sleep, at 9am I was still in the bag dozing when the take came. At first I couldn't understand what was happening; I was facing away from the lake after turning my brolly and, having finally found some sleep, felt very disorientated. Extracting myself from beneath the battered canopy, I ran towards the rods, all the time thinking 'tufty', even though I knew no bird alive could make the reel spin that fast. There was a fine, misty spray coming from the spool of the Emblem as the line rapidly disappeared out into the white-topped waves.

Jumping into the waders, I splashed out towards the rods and carefully tightened down to the fast-moving fish. As the 3lb rod took its full curve I realised, with some shock, that I was in fact attached to a carp! A 20-minute battle among the waves was a heart-stopping, but fitting, part of the script and when a big, grey mirror eventually rolled over the net cord I threw back my head and yelled in triumph!

By this point my waders were full of water where the waves had washed into me, but I cared not a jot as I squelched ashore clasping my prize. The best part was yet to come though – laying the carp down I drew back the mesh and identified the fish as none other than Speckles – uncaught for five years! The weight of 29lb 5oz was academic, I was ecstatic and totally made up with my first Pit Two carp; the fact that it was such a rare one made it all the sweeter.

I didn't have to pack up for a few hours and things still looked very good indeed. A new rig and fresh, oily pop-up was quickly recast to the same spot. As I felt the lead down with a thump, a good mirror rolled over among the waves, just yards from where the cast landed. No freebies were required!

I was under the brolly at 1pm, tidying the kit away for the journey back to the car, when the same thing happened to the right-hand rod, positioned at the bottom of the shelf. This time the take was even faster and for a while I thought I was playing a true monster. It went and went and went before eventually tiring and coming back towards me fairly quietly. When I finally netted it I was a bit surprised to see a less-than-massive carp nestling in the mesh. The fish turned out to be the character known as Little Shoulders at 23lb 4oz. A brace was more than I could ever have hoped for and was a very rare Pit Two occurrence indeed.

Memorable Trip

My next weekend session wasn't until almost the middle of August, but little did I know it was going to be another memorable trip. After a lengthy walk, I eventually found a small group of mirrors patrolling an area around a sunken island, just down the bank from the main snags. The largest of the group was the awe-inspiring Epaulettes at well over 35lb, and after a lot of ground-level manoeuvring through the bushes and brambles I was able to get right up close with some bait and a rod. Within a short while I had managed to get the big mirror feeding confidently on a couple of handfuls of casters right in the edge – literally within inches of the bank. The water was only two feet deep and gin clear. Mesmerised, I watched the great plated back of the fish as it eagerly hoovered up the crunchy grubs. After just a few minutes she had cleared the lot and slowly moved out of the swim, disappearing into a 'shiny' area of water up to my right that my polarising glasses couldn't quite see into.

"Making the most of my window of opportunity, I quickly lowered the rig – a 2oz inline lead and a single tiger nut – onto the spot. It sat perfectly, the leadcore leader following the contours of the shelf, with the limp line hanging off the rod tip. It seemed like I couldn't fail. At that point, and without warning, the fish known as Epaulettes appeared and cruised into the baited area at my feet."

Making the most of my window of opportunity, I quickly lowered the rig – a 2oz inline lead and a single tiger nut – onto the spot. It sat perfectly, the leadcore leader following the contours of the shelf, with the limp line hanging off the rod tip. At that point it seemed like I couldn't fail.

The coast was still clear, so I took the opportunity to place a small handful of casters straight on top of the rig, just to prime it all back up again. At that very moment, totally without warning, Epaulettes appeared from the shiny area and cruised back to the baited area at my feet. The casters had already left my hand, but had not yet hit the surface of the water; everything happened in slow motion and I wished I could somehow press rewind and suck them all back into my palm before they peppered the still surface of the margin. I can still see her clearly, five years later, the memory embedded in my minds' eye. She slowly swam through a shower of casters with them rolling off her back and trickling down her flanks. Emerging nonchalantly the other side of the bait shower, she erected all her fins in defiance and powerfully kicked off out into the deeps… it took me a while to get over that encounter!

High Pressure

I was pleased that something was happening every time I went to the pit and felt that my next chance wouldn't be too far away. I was able to fish all of the following weekend and it was typical late-August weather – high pressure, hot and still. In fact, it was perfect for floaters and, after some persistence, I managed to get a group of eight fish feeding confidently on the surface. The largest was clearly Lisa; identifiable due to the thick white mucus along her dorsal line – she looked big all right and although she wouldn't go near the hook bait she tried to eat the controller, twice!

Having watched the carp feeding for a few hours and been unable to get a take, I took a closer look at my set-up to see what might be at fault. It was a basic rig consisting of a long Double Strength hook link, a size 10 hook and a 10g controller attached to floating, braided main line. It is the same set-up I use everywhere, but something about it was unacceptable to these Elstow carp. After watching the carp carefully, I came to the conclusion that they were wary of the braided main line; they were reluctant to pass under it and it generally made them quite spooky. I had never found this to be a problem before, even in similarly clear water, but decided to tie in a Double Strength leader, about two rod lengths long, to keep the braid away from the carp.

As it happened, the action came to a close and the fish drifted away. However, on the Sunday I located a group of fish off the road bank, cruising on the surface over very deep water. After a while I managed to get them feeding. One of them was very big indeed and must have been either The Twin or The Mother – it was taking the odd floater too!

The change to the floater presentation seemed to do the job and on my first cast I was into a fish. After a great scrap I landed my third Elstow carp in as many weeks – this one was a mirror known as The Peach and I recorded a weight of 18lb 8oz.

The following session was a disappointment and I managed to ruin two good chances on floaters, pulling out of one big fish on the strike. Despite this, I was well aware just how many chances my mobile and varied tactics were producing – I just needed a little more luck and I felt that one of the big ones would come my way.

Blue Cliffs Of Dover

At the beginning of September the weather broke and we were treated to a new, fresh northerly wind that was blowing strongly into an area known as 'The Cliffs of Dover'. I set up in the teeth of it and put some bait out onto some nice-feeling spots – it really did look good for a take. I did periodically walk all the way around the pit to check the main snags – I felt that one or two carp might try and take advantage of the warmth on the back of the wind. It was 'one last look' on the Sunday lunchtime before I finally saw one; the unmistakable white dorsal area catching my eye as a big, grey mirror crossed an area of open water between the snags and the big weed bed. It was Lisa, alone and looking quite up for it. Never the gentleman, I was only too keen to take advantage of her.

Running back around the pit (which is a long way), I grabbed my floater rod and bait before running all the way back again. Thinking of this makes me realise how much fitter I must have been then. All the time that I was running along the dusty track I was praying that she would still be there. As I arrived back, from the top of the cliff I could see the great back below me. Traversing carefully down the bank, I positioned myself behind a small gorse bush. I fired out a pouchful of floaters past the fish and began to rig up the rod. Knowing how finicky they could be, I decided to tie up a long hair so that I could fish two baits with around an inch gap between them. On the surface they looked perfect – just like two freebies floating closely together.

Looking up, I saw a big pair of shoulders rise in the water as the first floater disappeared. I sent the tiny controller out past the carp, feathering it so that it landed with an almost inaudible plop. Slowly I wound it back until the hook bait was directly in her path. Hardly able to breath, I watched and waited as the shoulders moved closer to the hook bait, engulfing every bait without hesitation. More and more floaters disappeared… then, like nothing I have ever seen before, the fish rose even higher in the water and just seemed to collapse down on top of the hook bait. I half expected the strike to send the controller sailing past my shoulder, but no, this was my moment.

The fish turned, confusedly floundered for a moment and then set off on the most unstoppable run, straight along the side of the headlands. The lip of the spool was burning into my fingertips as I tried without success to slow it down. I paced it out along the headlands later on and found that the fish travelled more than 70 yards on its first run! There was little I could do on such light tackle but hang on and pray it would run out of steam. It was out over deep, weed-and-snag-free water; the danger would come when I bought the fish back to the snags close in front of me. Hopefully, by then it would be behaving itself a little better.

Eventually, after a heart-stopping battle, I regained all the line and had the fish under the rod tip. I stood, up to my waist in water and could clearly see her twisting and turning in the deep, crystal-clear margin. The soft-actioned rod was absorbing the fish's power and, slowly, I felt she was tiring. One of the regulars, Martin, had heard my yells for help and had come around to lend a hand, positioning the net and waiting patiently for me to bring the carp up. After what seemed an age, the fish was finally beaten and Lisa rolled over the net cord. The tiny size 10 fell out in the net, but it didn't matter – it had done its job and the fish was mine.

We recorded a weight of 36lb 6oz; a new personal best and a new surface record for the lake. That capture topped off a challenging, frustrating and at times exhilarating acquaintance with Pit Two and its tricky stock of mirrors. Perhaps strangely, I have never returned, getting sidetracked by some Thames carp. However, one day I will almost certainly return…

"I regained some line and stood, up to my waist in water. I could clearly see her twisting and turning in the deep, crystal-clear margin."

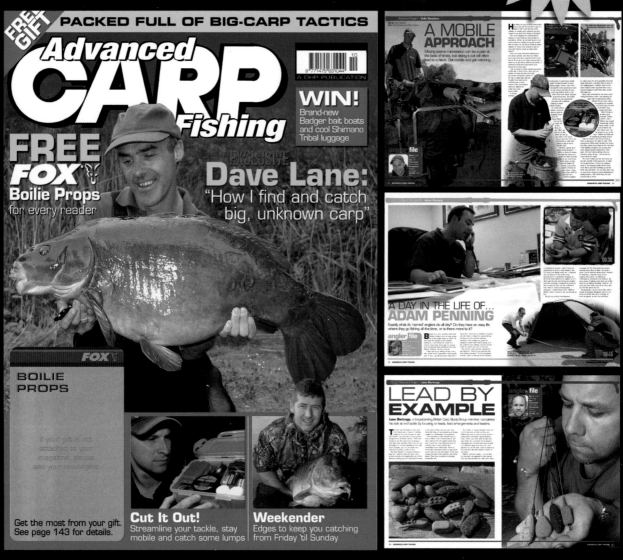

Leads, we've got them covered .... even the swivels!

NEW FOR 2005

from 99p

The new Fox carp lead range has been designed to create the optimum profiles for both aerodynamics and bolt rig efficiency. Each lead is then formed with precision injection moulding to provide perfect form and shape consistency throughout the range. A special rubberised coating is then applied which creates a subtle, non-reflective finish. This is highly durable, non reflective and inconspicuous on the lakebed which blends in perfectly with most surroundings.

The In-Line leads feature a special one piece Safety Sleeve which securely grips a size 7 Fox swivel, allowing the lead to pull free and slide off in the event of a jam or breakage. This creates a streamlined and tangle free lead system that can be safely used with leadcore, tubing or shockleaders without modification.

The New Fox Leads Range available in single and twin packs

The entire lead is coated – including the swivel and the loop. Every loop is consistently formed and inserted to the correct depth in the lead. The swivels and loops are smooth, clean and free from excess coating.

Each swivel lead is designed to work with any lead clip without modification. The eye of each swivel is enlarged to fit Fox Carp Safety Clips, and if preffered, the swivel can be removed and the mounted directly onto the clip.

- Flat Pear
- Tri Bomb
- Kling On

Available in both swivel and in-line versions and in quarter ounce increments to suit any rod test curve and all possible rig requirements.

- Horizon
- Elevator

FOX

www.foxint.com

ON SALE IN FOX STOCKISTS NOW!

Mere Memories

The multi-talented Gareth Fareham recounts the story of two awesome Cheshire carp...

Being brought up fishing in the north, there was one place you always heard about on the grapevine and of all the lakes in this neck of the woods Redesmere takes the honours for the most notorious, hands down. Situated right in the heart of a leafy and affluent part of Cheshire, on the estate of Bromley Davenport, it is a typically ancient-looking mere, surrounded by gnarled old fallen trees, farmland and densely wooded areas, it really is a truly beautiful lake. At the time, it was home to some of the biggest and most famous carp in the north but the spates of tackle thefts and car break-ins, cliquey regulars, difficult rules and a history for being ridiculously busy, all added to its moody reputation and, to be honest, coming off the quiet little estate lakes I was used to, it was hardly the most inviting of places. The stories of lads queuing behind each other for days to get in a going swim were enough to put anyone off but the fishing itself also had an unwelcoming reputation. It seemed that blank years weren't all that uncommon and half a dozen a season was a right result, any captures from the Mere were regarded as hard won, that's for sure.

Secret Squirrels

I didn't know any of the lads who were fishing over on the Mere, so I only ever got to hear little snippets about what was coming out or how busy it was. Occasionally you might hear that 'the common' had been caught and how big it was but conversations never went much further. It wasn't spoken about in hushed tones as such, but it did seem to be a closed circle of information unless you actually fished there; or at least had mates that did. It was busy enough so why make it any busier by encouraging others I suppose?

Funnily enough though, it was that element of secrecy that made the place so captivating for me. The prestige of the fish and the fact that they were so highly regarded also held a big appeal for me. I wanted a little piece of Cheshire carp fishing history and there was no better place to get that than Redesmere.

The Stock

As for the fish, the initial stockings were in1958 and 1964 and by now they were as ancient looking as the lake itself. It held a number of particularly pretty mirrors and the two big commons.

The Male was a long, dark chestnut-coloured fish which at its biggest had been out at just under 39lb and looked set to do forty. The Snub was a much shorter, younger-looking fish with an incredibly thick wrist and a lovely rounded nose and was generally in the 34lb to 36lb range

The Male was the first fish I ever really set out to target and at the time, in the mid-late 1990s, there weren't that many bigger commons in the country, which made it even more of a worthy target.

I actually carried a little photo of it around with me when I started on the Mere

"The Male was the first fish I ever set out to target and, at the time, there weren't that many bigger commons in the country."

just to remind myself why I was there during the slow periods. In 1997, as a 16-year-old keenie, it all seemed a bit of a lofty dream. After all, there had been lads fishing up there for 10 years or more that hadn't caught it, so what made me think I had a chance? I was following in the footsteps of some brilliant anglers.

Lads like Bernie Loftus, Frank Warwick, Graham Trickett, the Seals, Andy Cooper and Paul Selman had all done their time on the Mere and, when I finally did buy a ticket, the prospect of actually fishing the place was really quite inspiring.

Now, although I didn't exactly take it apart that first year, I did manage to get three bites, which was a result in itself, the first being one of the big, known mirrors called Single Scale at 33lb 12oz. Getting that first bite and getting off the mark spurred me on massively. I knew if I could catch one then I could catch more and when I managed a mid-twenty the following week I thought I had the place sussed. That was August... soon it was September, then October and November passed without incident and before I knew it I'd done a six-month blank. I only actually saw another two on the bank during that period, too!

This was more like it. The fishing certainly lived up to its reputation but as for the cliquey locals... all a hoax; the social aspect of the Mere was brilliant. I've never met a sounder bunch of anglers in my life and they're all my best mates now! Being skint, and always fishing instead of working, let's just say I was never too well stocked with supplies but the lads always looked after me and kept me fed and watered when I was running low or had decided to stay on for an extra night or two. Not having my own wheels, I also ponced more than the occasional lift too!

No Illusions

I stayed on and did the winter that first year. With well over 50 nights between my second fish in August and my third in February I finished the season with my tail stuffed firmly between my legs.

I was under no illusions about how difficult it was going to be.

All that time and effort certainly wasn't wasted though, and I learnt some important lessons during all those blanks, especially through winter when it was quiet and I could get a feel for the areas properly.

I regrouped and came back the following year with a proper game plan and the old, dog-eared photo of the common still tucked away in a pocket of my rucksack. That was definitely the one I wanted.

I fished hard and hooked 25 carp that next summer, landing 16 of them.

However, with all the bigger fish eluding me I was more fired up than ever to see one on the bank.

Chris with The Male at 36lb 6oz back in the summer of 2002. That really was a stunning carp and a real pedigree fish.

Charles with an upper 20. All my best mates are lads I met on Redesmere – the socials were something special!

Bri 'the miner' with the Original Linear off The Meadow. A top angler and a top bloke, always with a tale to tell.

I checked my watch and it was after midnight. I'd fished the weekend, been home and was back again – I was in need of some sleep!

Autumn Harvest

I had to go back to college in September but had decided to see a proper overnighter assault through until the frosts really kicked in, as it was a prime time for the big fish late in the year. It had already been worth the effort because I'd taken a mirror known as The Peach at 30lb 2oz in September on one of them, but since then I'd gone three or four weeks without a bite.

It was late October and the long-range areas off The Snag and Stream had been the most consistent areas over the preceding few weeks. I hadn't been able to get anywhere near them though, as they'd been more or less permanently occupied.

The weeknights were my only chance of getting in the area. I'd fished an overnighter in the Left-Hand Holly on the Tuesday night and saw a good fish head and shoulder out in no-man's land off The Snag, just as I was packing up. I hadn't planned to do the Wednesday night but seeing that fish perked me up a bit and I came straight back down from college hoping to drop in there. Luckily, The Snag was free. If it hadn't have been I was just going to turn straight around and head home. A real icy-cold southeasterly had sprung up during the day and I remember standing out in my chest waders, freezing, having to blow on my hands after every cast while I was putting some bait out and wondering why on earth I was bothering. It all felt so futile, especially as the few fish that were getting caught were coming out during the day.

Finally, just before dark, I'd got them lashed out and a bit of bait scattered in the area. I'd barely sorted myself and got the stove fired up to get some blood back into my fingers when I had a drop-back. A bream and a turned hook point was the decidedly unexciting result… a new rig, balanced 'nouvelle' hook bait and 20 minutes later the scenario repeated itself… and then again shortly after. Eventually, I managed to get in my bag and get my head down. On checking my watch, it was just after midnight. I'd done the weekend, had spent Monday night at home, and then been straight back down for the last two nights, so I desperately needed some sleep. My tutors were starting to get a bit twitchy about me literally falling asleep in lessons.

The next thing I knew I was coming around to the high-pitched scream of a Neville and a little red LED glowing at me out in the blackness. It seemed to take an age to fumble into my chesties; all the while I could just hear my clutch going. The fight was heavy and I remember thinking from the start it felt like a good 'un. The sky had cleared by now to leave a big, bright moon and a starry sky and the relentless wind had finally given up. After a long, dogged fight out at range, eventually it was beaten and gulped a mouthful of air. I lifted under the silver reflections in the black, inky swirl – missing it completely! After a last 20-yard run I made no mistakes the second time around.

Feeling down into the net I put my hand on its shoulders and realised it was a big fish. I laughed excitedly to myself, thinking how I should have been at home in bed and not out here alone with the stars and a carp. I didn't have my torch so it wasn't until I'd waded back to the bank that I could identify exactly which common it was.

Cheshire History

There on my mat lay The Original Linear, probably the best-looking fish in the lake and quite possibly one of the Leney's from the initial Surrey farm stocking in 1958. A proper little bit of Cheshire history and on a weeknight too, I was buzzing! That was my last action of the year and I fished on until it closed on March 14th without another bite.

It was late May of 1999 and the road bank at Redesmere was filled with forty odd carp anglers all awaiting the draw for the start of the season. As long as I came out higher than my 38th from the previous year I'd be happy but, like everyone else, I was really hoping to come out early. The usual pre-season banter was rife and there was a real buzz. The first week of the season on the Mere is generally really productive, and one or two of the big 'uns almost always get caught. However, with the bulk of the carp making the most of the fresh weed growth in the shallows and in front of the yacht club, it had narrowed the potential producing spots down to maybe only half a dozen. If you got a bad draw you were buggered basically! Although there were a lot of fish right down in the shallows, there was a big low pressure forecast, potentially bringing some serious rain with it. I had a feeling they probably wouldn't stay there

"After a long, dogged fight at range, it was beaten and gulped a mouthful of air. I lifted the net under the silver reflections in the inky swirl... and missed! After landing it, I felt down into the net and laughed at myself, thinking how I should have been at home in bed and not out here alone. It wasn't until I'd waded back that I could identify the fish. Soon, on my mat, lay the Original Linear, probably the best-looking fish in the lake and quite possibly one of the Leney's from the initital Surrey farm stocking in 1958. A proper little bit of Cheshire history – I was buzzing!"

Over 40 years old and a little piece of Cheshire carp fishing history – the stunning Original Linear. I felt so lucky to have joined the list of anglers to tread the banks of Redesmere and to have caught such wonderful fish as this one.

Ship ahoy! There was plenty going on at Redesmere apart from the carp fishing. We had a bit to contend with.

for long, especially when a few leads started landing on top of their heads.

I'd been down regularly over the last few weeks and knew the area I wanted to be in. However, it was Gav who came out first and chose Bluebells, a wise decision I thought, as that was my first choice. The Wide and The Front went next and, lo and behold, I came out next, opting for the 4th swim on the New Bank in the hope that I could get in behind Gav after the initial 48 hours. In effect 'wasting' my first two days. Although it's an awkward rule, the 48-hour maximum does stop areas being stitched up for any length of time. Bluebells had been a really consistent area the year before, with both the big commons being caught from there on a couple of occasions, and I wanted to get in there that first week. Everyone headed down to the Blacksmith's after the draw and, after talking the season away over a few pints, Flinty dropped me home later that day.

Dark Skies

I arrived the evening before the start to find the road bank deserted, the rain had put an untimely stop to any social activities and it seemed everyone was already tucked away under their brollies. The sky was dark and heavy and despite only being 6pm it felt more like 10. I trudged my way up the footpath, across the road and down through the fields to the New Bank, getting wetter by the minute. The long, unkempt grass soaked everything.

The first 48 hours passed uneventfully and most of it was spent hiding from the relentless rain under Gav's Titan talking his ear off, drinking his tea and eating all his biscuits. A few fish had started to show out in the main body, on the end of the northwesterly that had sprung up, and everyone's first-week plans went out of the window. I decided to stick with mine, I'd seen a couple show in Bluebells and, although it wasn't ideal, I still felt it was worth a shout. Gav packed up, I moved in, and everyone else did their own version of musical bivvies.

Conditions were miserable; it was still

"It really was dark and, not having a torch with me, I struggled to see anything while playing the fish. I shouted to Oggy, who was next door in the 4th swim, but got no reply. Little did I know that he sleeps like a dead man!"

raining, the lake was actually starting to flood and the swim was a quagmire. I got sorted quickly and by early evening my baits were in position on a nice hard spot, on the edge of the huge expanse of weed, in front of the yacht club. Crawling under my crippled brolly, I got out of the waders and the clinging mud and lay on my bag, exhausted. I must have dozed off, because next thing I knew both rods were literally being ripped off my set-up as a yacht ploughed through my swim and both my lines! No time for the chesties and I cursed myself for having fallen asleep as I stood there covered in mud and up to my waist in water, cupping both spools in a vain attempt to ping them off the dagger board. Eventually they did, but not before the rigs had been dragged through 30 odd yards of 'forest'. It must have taken me a good half an hour to haul the rigs and rafts of weed in. Oh man, why me?

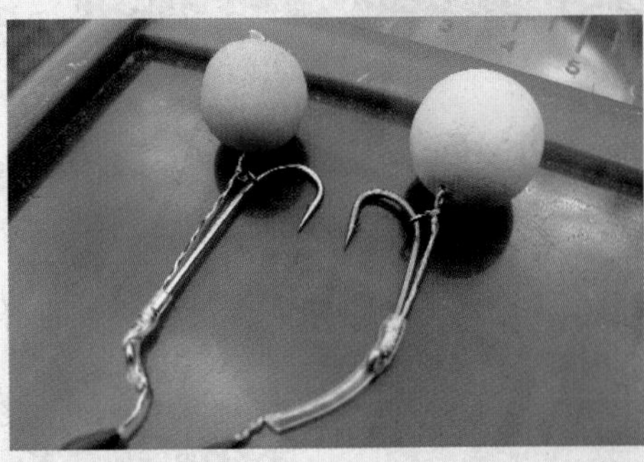

My favourite presentation back then (left) has changed little since, apart from the components. Good rigs are good rigs.

The line was trashed, so a good 70 yards was stripped off both and I started from scratch. It was getting darker by the minute and, as I'd lost all my tape markers for the spot, I needed to get them out in the light; otherwise it'd be a gamble I didn't want to take. I managed to get them back out nicely and, just after I'd got the second rod in, a big black set of head and shoulders lifted out, smack on the spot.

I was soaked to the skin by now and, as it was almost dark, I just stripped off and crawled into my bag. I slept fitfully, as everything was wet; and even though it was June, I was bloody freezing. The incessant drumming of the rain on my brolly added insult to injury and kept me awake.

The Male

Sometime in the early hours I had a take and, before I knew it, I was stood out in the darkness up to my waist in water playing a fish. It was still raining heavily and one of those blacker-than-black nights because of the low cloud. From the outset it was obvious it was a good fish and every time I gained some line another heavy, determined run took it all back. Slowly it kited around to my left on a long line and eventually bogged down in some heavy weed up the margin. Leaning into it, I gave it as much as I dared, knowing I had to keep it moving at all costs. If it stopped it probably wouldn't have started again. By now I was just pumping a dead weight and only the occasional dull thud reassured me the fish was still on, the line grating horribly down through the maze of weed beds. It really was dark and, not having a torch on me, I was struggling to see anything at all, I shouted to Oggy who was next door in the 4th swim but got no reply – little did I know he sleeps like a dead man. Eventually I got a huge raft of weed to the net but, no matter how hard I tried, I just couldn't lift the arms under it all – it was probably twice the size of the net. The next thing I knew the rod was almost torn from my hand as I touched the fish with the cord. It went ballistic, tearing off down the margin and flat-rodding me. With the line jerking down at a 90-degree angle through the raft, all it needed was one of the little zebra mussels in the weed to nick the line and it would've all been over.

Bit by bit I gained all the line back and after doing my best to clear some of the weed, with the fish wallowing around, I dropped the rod and somehow bundled everything into the net, blind… what a nightmare!

Reaching down, I felt the width of the fish and the distinctive, slightly 'rough' scales of a common. There were only two of that size in the Mere and The Snub was a cleaner common, I knew it was The Male before I even saw it. Yessssss! I shouted Oggy again… still no answer.

Standing there in the blackness and rain I just took it all in for a minute or two before wading back to the bank to sort it all out.

It went 34lb15oz on the scales and, although a bit down in weight, it was in immaculate condition and looked stunning. In the difficult conditions Oggy did me a sterling job with the photos. It had taken three years of hard work and an untold number of nights but, with The Male on the mat at my knees, I realised I'd accomplished my dream, an ambition achieved and one I'll remember forever.

How could I ever forget, in fact? The long nights, painful blanks, hard work and sheer determination all made for a fascinating campaign.

I had some great times on Redesmere, and made a lot of very good friends, many of which remain friends today. They all, as well as the awesome carp, made my time on Redesmere a very enjoyable one.

The quality of the fish I caught was testimony to the quality of the angler that fished for them. The respect that the Mere carp were shown is an absolute credit to those lucky enough to fish on the place. The Male was immaculate when I caught it and was 23lb when I was born back in 1980.

RIP Fellas

That June was the last time I ever saw the common. Being such an old fish it never quite did make forty in the seasons after I left and I'd heard that last season it had started to drop back in weight, getting caught looking quite ill at 26lb and then 24lb, and then sadly finally turning up dead just a few months ago

The Original Linear is another of the Redesmere originals that has passed away recently.

At more than 40 years old they were part of an important legacy of the northwest scene and had gone a long way to shaping the history of fishing in the area and touched a lot of anglers' hearts along the way. I for one, along with many others I'm sure, am truly glad that I fished the place while they were still in their prime and had the chance to share a few precious moments with them.

RIP fellas and thanks for the memories.

> **"I for one, along with many others I'm sure, am truly glad that I fished the place while they were still in their prime and had the chance to spend a few precious moments with them. RIP fellas and thanks for the memories."**

Watching surface-cruising carp on a warm summer's afternoon – awesome.

Horton Haulin'

The famous Horton Church Lake was the scene of a magical floater fishing campaign for big-fish maestro Jim Shelley...

I first recognised the potential of Horton as a floater fishing venue when, on a trip in 2004, I decided to tackle up with just a spod rod and floater fishing rod and a small amount of terminal tackle that I might need for the day.

Unbeknown to me at the time, one or two of the regulars had been feeding floaters and getting the fish feeding. I had been there one day and saw these carp on the surface and they seemed to be feeding quite confidently. This was purely down to the fact that the boys had done so well in getting them to accept the floating baits. Like I said though, I didn't know that at the time, I just saw loads of carp that looked well catchable, so decided that it would be rude not to have a go! Nobody had managed to catch anything off the surface yet and I was determined that I was going to give it my best shot.

Armed with my two rods, tackle, unhooking mat and a considerable amount of dog biscuits, 25kg in fact, I set off around the lake early one morning. It was only a few weeks into the season and the weather was absolutely bang on for a bit of floater action.

On my first trip down I found some carp that looked well up for a floater or two.

That session turned into a bit of a successful one, to say the least. I spent a couple of days chasing fish around the lake and managed to land a 34lb mirror and a 37lb grass carp, as well as losing a few and missing a few good chances.

That brief spell down there taught me a few things and added another piece to the carp fishing jigsaw. I knew that there would be a certain time of the year when I fancied my chances on Horton for a surface carp or two.

I fish a few different waters each year and time my campaigns on there to when I think my chances are at their highest.

For instance, when I target the Road Lake I am confident that a window of opportunity presents itself around February/March time. That's when my chances are best, so that is when I approach the water. It has worked so far, and this is just one example of that timing element of my carp fishing.

I'd got a lot going on in my private life, so that first floater effort at Horton was cut short. However, I knew that I could get down there the following year and I'd have a chance of some floater fishing.

At the time, it seemed almost nothing more than a date in my diary, but it was to prove a very effective decision.

Horton Return

So it was that I returned in the early part of the season in 2005. I got down to the lake, armed only with the essentials, and set about having a bit of a wander around the pond. I saw fish in just about every area of the lake – there were fish everywhere!

There are a good number of stockies in Horton these days – carp that have been introduced by RMC (CEMEX as it is known now), and they all appeared up for a bit of a surface munch.

I have watched these fish progress from their first stocking right up until now. At the time of this visit there were several over 35lb, with the biggest being recorded at around 43lb.

I made my way into the swim known as The Ski Slope. The morning had begun brightly but then I remember a distinct change in the conditions. The wind had got up and was blowing quite a brisk southwesterly and a bank of cloud had moved in.

In the ripple, well it was more than a ripple, the fish seemed to disappear. I do know that they like that end of the lake, around Church Bay and Dog Bay, especially when the wind was blowing in that direction, and especially out of Springate's. It's a big chuck out to the middle there and the carp always seemed to turn up there first.

After an hour or two of watching the water, I noticed the telltale sign of grass carp. They have a very distinct dorsal fin, almost a V shape, and I could see one or two taking my mixers off the surface. I'd fed mixers on the wind and let them drift into the area where I suspected the carp were.

Telltale Swirls

Grassies are often the first on the case and they do like a floater. A lot of anglers find the grassies to be nothing more than a nuisance. I don't mind catching them, but I do not target them. However, they do play a key role in this sort of fishing, so I don't mind them being in the swim. Where there are grassies there will often be carp as well, so it's not always a bad sign.

I noticed one or two grassies, and their telltale swirls, so I carried on spodding mixers out. It's always difficult getting mixers out at range, so spodding helps enormously. I am talking about feeding at over 100 yards here, and I have found the spod the only effective way of doing this. I can get a lot of floaters out there in a short space of time, and at range, with a spod. I cannot do that by firing PVA bags of floaters out with the catapult.

"I use a lot of floaters, many of which are 'wasted'. By this I mean that they feed off all the gulls, ducks, swans and anything else that might help themselves. If I didn't do this, the carp would get little or none."

There is a knack to delivering floaters with the spod. A spod is obviously semi-buoyant, with the nose cone being the most buoyant part. Floaters are also buoyant so it doesn't necessarily follow that the spod will turn over as it normally would.

Just before the spod hits the surface I hit the line hard and the mixers empty out on the surface. This also creates a lot less disturbance on the water, even though that's not the primary reason behind me doing it.

I keep the spod going out there regularly and create what I call my chum line. This refers to when sea anglers put chum out and let it drift in a line, attracting fish up and towards their bait.

I use a large amount of mixers and many are wasted. By this, I mean that the carp do not get to eat them. However, these 'extra' baits feed off the gulls, ducks, swans and whatever else might be helping themselves at the time. If I only put a few out, the birds would massacre these and the carp would get little or none of them.

The gulls at Horton, as anyone who has fished there will confess, are ridiculous and it can be a nightmare avoiding their attentions. I just feed them off with loads of bait – simple!

Feeding Zone

As I started to get the carp feeding and taking a few mixers, a chap walked past behind me. I want to protect what I have created in this feeding zone and I am wary of his intentions. I wondered where he might be heading.

This can be a nightmare. I won't mention any names but there were definitely a few 'followers' on there at the time. They don't

The effort was paying off as I started to land a few nice ones like this one – Cossack – and Uno (right) at 37lb.

really know what they are doing and rely on you to do the legwork for them.

I don't mean this in any detrimental way at all, it's just that I had worked hard to get them going and now it looked like someone else might reap the rewards. I am not even saying that they necessarily do it on purpose. In fact, I think that often they don't.

Anyway, this chap stopped at my swim.

"Hello Jim," he pipes up. "I see you've got 'em going. You don't mind if I drop in next door do you?" he asks.

It was my worst nightmare. The wind had died somewhat and the sun was out again. There was a drift, or current, on the water and many of the mixers were making their way back to my right and to the swim that he went into. The swims here are very tight and this fella then proceeded to spod out some mixers, but further out than he could cast a controller.

My baits were drifting in front of him, but I could not cast over there, as this was now his water. I'd been working the area with a view to going next door if this exact thing should occur. I couldn't do this now as he was in the swim.

I'd spent the best part of three hours getting the fish feeding. There was now an angler in the very next swim, not even a couple of swims down, who was now going to take advantage of all my efforts.

However, I accept that this is often part of carp fishing and you just have to get on with it.

Floater fishing is an exhausting tactic, both mentally and physically. There are so many things against you that it is so easy to just not bother. The fact that fish are cagey feeders on the surface, the bird life, the 'followers', the heat, changing winds, these are all things that go against you.

However, you have to persevere if you are going to be successful. The floater angler is a dedicated soul and that's the way it has to be.

I travel very light, get up at the crack of dawn, and spend the whole day giving it 100 per cent. I only carry the essential tackle, my bait and a bottle or two of water. As long as I can drink and take a leak, that's all I need! I don't even answer my mobile; in fact I switch it off most of the time. I am absolutely committed to it and will do what I have to in order to increase my chances. It's hard, but it brings its results. I think this level of effort is why so many carp anglers choose not to fish on the surface as much as they could.

I get such a buzz from floater fishing – I absolutely love it, but it is hard work. It's not like sitting behind three rods on sticks. It happens there, right in front of you, and you can see the fish actually eating your baits. That is a great thing to see and I love it.

The carp gods looked down on me that day

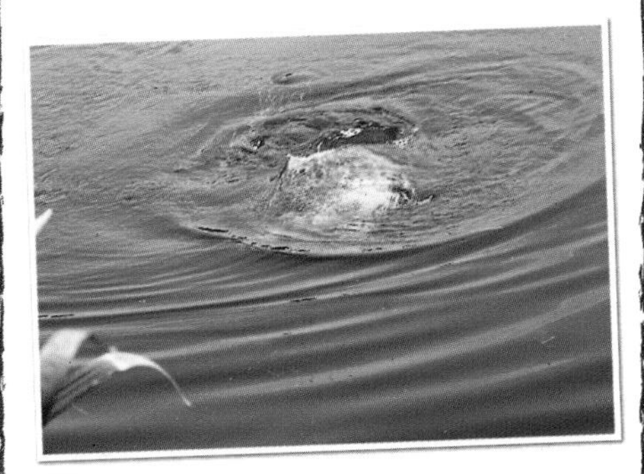

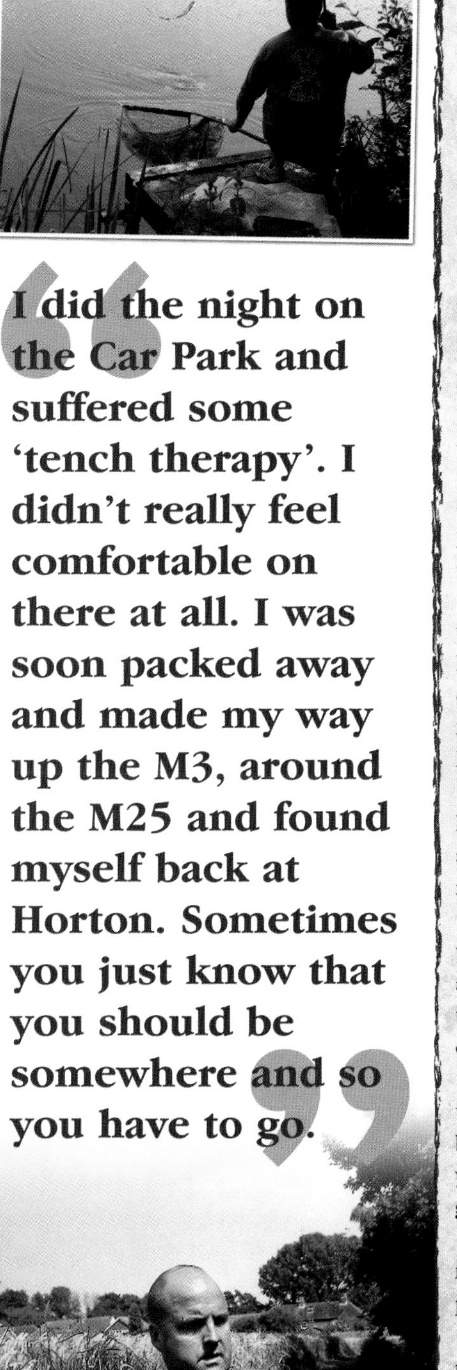

"I did the night on the Car Park and suffered some 'tench therapy'. I didn't really feel comfortable on there at all. I was soon packed away and made my way up the M3, around the M25 and found myself back at Horton. Sometimes you just know that you should be somewhere and so you have to go."

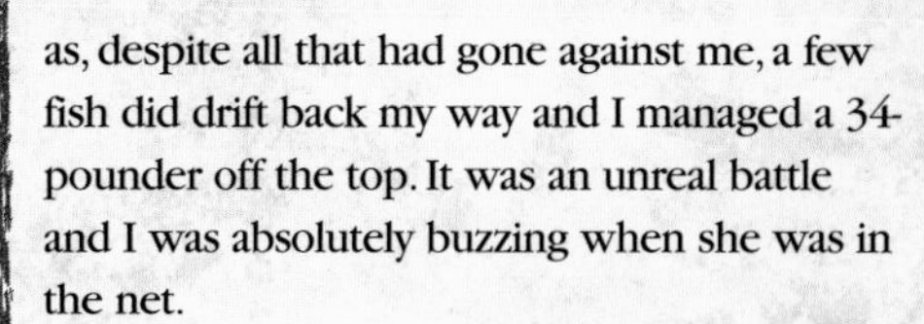

as, despite all that had gone against me, a few fish did drift back my way and I managed a 34-pounder off the top. It was an unreal battle and I was absolutely buzzing when she was in the net.

It was a fish called Cossack and I had worked my socks off to catch it. It was one very satisfying catch.

Commited, 100 Per Cent

I returned the next day, but it passed pretty much without incident, so I was back home again that night, still high on the anticipation of what was still to come.

I had a few days 'off' and didn't fish for the rest of that week. I have a life outside of fishing and it is very important to me. While I am on the bank I am 100 per cent committed to it, but when I am at home I enjoy the pleasure of my family's company.

On the Sunday of that week though, I was ready to go angling again. I made my way to Yateley Car Park Lake and was soon fishing in the Bars swim. I knew that if it didn't go to plan down there I could easily make my way down to Horton, if the conditions were right for a bit of floater fishing.

I sat back, after having put a bit of bait out, and relaxed in front of the portable DVD player that my fiancée had bought me that Christmas.

I say relax, but I didn't feel too relaxed. I had the feeling that I didn't want to really be there. It's an odd place and I do not always feel that comfortable on the Car Park. I knew that the fish were in the weed bed opposite, and I also knew that I could not get to them.

I only really want one fish out of the Car Park, so I don't feel drawn to it like some anglers do. It is a magical place, I suppose, but it's not always for me.

I did the night and got my share of 'tench therapy'! I was tired and didn't stir until around 9am. I got up and had a wander about the swim and thought to myself: "What am I doing here?"

I was soon packed away and made my way up the M3, around the M25 and found myself back at Horton. Sometimes you just know that you should be somewhere and so you have to go.

I was back, conditions were good, and I felt a huge relief that I was in the right place.

I threw the essentials into the unhooking mat. Tackle, loads of mixers, camera, scales, a drink and a packet of crisps – they all went in. I could have sat there, vegging away at Yateley, but I made my way down here, signed in and was ready to go.

I was soon in the Scooter swim, in an area in between the chop of the wind and the calmer leeward area.

I have noticed that the Horton carp do not

When playing this carp I was convinced that it was one of the small commons, so wanted to land it and recast as quickly as possible. I was so wrong, as it turned out to be Pimple, a Longfield original!

The fish known as Tiger, at 29lb 15oz. I like to catch thirties, of course I do, but you have to be honest with the scales. This was another very welcome capture.

like to take mixers in the area where the wind is really rippling, but they do like the area on the wind line. I am not sure why this is but I have definitely noticed a tendency for them to do so.

I got the spod out and started putting some baits out. Some people don't like the spod going out and think it creates unnecessary disturbance. I actually think that at Horton the carp come to the sound of the spod and recognise it as signalling the arrival of food. It's like the old adage of it being like a dinner bell, well, at Horton it's true.

Game On!

Contrary to floater fishing folklore, I get my controller out there quickly. I have had fish feeding when I have been retrieving my spod from the very first cast, so why not have the hook bait out there nice and early.

Anyway, within 20 minutes or so I hooked and landed a 25lb leather, despite its very best efforts to smash me in the weed. Game on!

As Gary Lewis took the photos for me, he was telling me how there were carp out there absolutely gorging themselves on my floaters. I was desperate to get the controller back out there, so slipped the leather back safely and got back to work.

Within 30 seconds of my controller landing I was in again. My 2.75lb Pursuit rod immediately took on its full test curve and I knew that this was a heavy fish. After a protracted battle, and a couple of hairy moments when the fish weeded me, I finally landed the fish they call Uno, at 37lb 8oz. I was so pleased that I'd left the Car Park. I was buzzing and the fish looked magnificent on the mat.

The remaining fish soon made their exit from the swim, but I was happy to play a bit of cat and mouse and follow them along.

A fish named Tiger, at 29lb 15oz, completed what was a memorable day and I was well pleased that I'd made the change of lakes.

I worked hard at those carp and had reaped the results. For all the occasions that floater fishing kicks you in the teeth, the successes more than make up for it.

I rewarded myself for my efforts with a nice bit of food and some alcohol-free beers before getting my head down in the lodge for the night.

"I cast the controller out beyond the fish. It landed strangely and the main line sank more than normal. It looked a bit wrong but I flicked some baits out anyway. They soon started taking them."

White Horses

The next morning the wind was causing quite a chop on the water. It had turned and was blowing more of an easterly direction to the day before. The waves were quite severe, although we're not talking white horses. However, there was a very choppy surface out there. I found some fish though, and for the only time ever I got them taking right in the choppy areas. They were having them, but not exactly big time. I sat for about five or six hours without a bite. I'd moved once or twice in that time and found myself in a swim with Springate's to my left and Church Bay to my right.

I hooked one and it took me all over the swim. I thought it was one of the smaller commons that like to have a tear up so I played it a bit more aggressively than I might a bigger carp. This isn't to say that I don't like catching smaller fish, far from it. I just knew that there were bigger carp in the swim and I wanted to get this one landed and returned so that I could get the hook bait back out there.

After 20 minutes, which I found a bit bizarre, the fish finally broke the surface and was netted. I was gobsmacked when I looked down on it. The fish I thought was a small common turned out to be an original Longfield common called Pimple at 34lb!

Later that day I found myself in the Ski Slope swim again. The wind seemed to be hacking through the swim, but a tree to my left seemed to just have an effect on one area that made the water look a bit 'different'. I spotted a carp over there taking some mixers that must have drifted in from somewhere. I flicked the controller out beyond the fish. It landed a bit strangely and, for some reason, the main line sank a little more than usual. This caused the float to sit a bit stiller than it would normally. It looked a bit wrong but I flicked some baits around it anyway. The carp soon started taking so I left it to see what happened.

It wasn't long before I had a take and I landed another 37-pounder. I couldn't believe my luck and was well pleased that I'd kept at it again. Nobody else was floater fishing and here I was snaffling up another chunk!

There was a storm that night, so I made an

extra-special effort to be up early the next day and take advantage of the fresh conditions.

A few more anglers had cottoned on and were floater fishing that morning. A couple had been caught down the other end, so the fish were tending to back up towards the lodge in search of a bit of sanctuary from the pressure. I worked and moved, worked and moved until I got some fish feeding confidently out in front of the swim known as The Blank. It was at long range and I was casting the controller at the limit of where I could get it.

After making a perfect cast to the back of the floaters, my phone went. It was a brief conversation as I was busy!

As I looked back round, I noticed the main line tighten slightly. I hit it and the rod was almost ripped from my hand. It took off like a grassie gone mad and it was soon over 150 yards away from me!

It was heading for Weedy Bay, over 200 yards away, and I was sure I was going to lose contact with it.

I steadily gave it some pressure and managed, briefly, to turn it. The beefy rod and reliable main line meant that I could get into a scrap with this fish and I soon gained a little more control. It gave me the right run around. But I managed to get myself on level terms with it and it became more of a fair fight. I was still convinced that it was a grassie, and had still not actually seen the fish.

My mate Dan had not long left me so, with the rod in one hand, I managed to ring him and ask him to come back and give me a hand. This was risky but I knew I was going to struggle to land it on my own.

I don't like playing carp on the surface and feel much more confident when they go deep. This fish did exactly that and I thought I had a good chance of landing it.

Dan arrived and made his way down to the water's edge with the net. I told him to keep the net deep, as the fish was doing likewise and I didn't want it to be spooked. Although I was still sure it was a grassie, you can't be too careful, especially after the incident with the common. Amazingly, and in a flash, Dan soon scooped the net under The Parrot – one of Horton's sought-after fish. I'd caught The Parrot before, off the bottom, but this was going to be new floater PB for me, so I didn't at all mind the repeat.

We weighed The Parrot at 44lb. It was indeed a new surface-caught PB and I was well pleased.

I knew, when asked, that this just had to be the story I related in this book, as it is one that will stay with me forever. I hope you have enjoyed reading it as much I did being there.

I know I'd caught The Parrot before, but tell me you wouldn't mind catching this one off the top, especially as it was a new surface PB at 44lb.

NY

The Secret Lake

Richard Farnan didn't need a second invitation when offered the chance to visit an unfished water in the south, whose stock is largely unknown. This is the stuff that dreams are made of...

Once in a lifetime an opportunity to fish a previously untapped lake for unknown carp may come along. For me such a journey began in January 2004.

Through a very good friend of mine, I was asked if I'd like to fish a private lake situated in the Wraysbury area for some unknown carp. I didn't need asking twice. A meeting was set up, with a chap I knew only as George, and a tour of the water was arranged.

After that first taste of the secret lake, on a cold January morning, I was eager to gather as much information about its history as possible. I was quite glad to find the information quite easy to obtain – when asking in the right places! The carp had been stocked into the lake between 1994 and 1996, in addition to any fish that may have already been present, which to date I am still unsure of. The carp were not originally meant for this pit, but had been stocked into a famous local lake. When introduced to the larger pit the carp averaged 4lb to 6lb. Some of the anglers that fished the large pit at the time were angling for some of the country's finest and largest carp and didn't appreciate these young 'uns being introduced.

> **We met up with the leaseholder who explained that there were only two rules. Night-fishing only, and to keep the place to ourselves!**

Stunning Mirrors

The majority of these smaller fish that were caught swiftly made there way into their new home. As far as we can gather, approximately 60 fish had been moved, mainly commons, but quite a few stunning mirrors were moved too. Since then they have been left to grow undisturbed.

We met the leaseholder of the lake that January morning, who explained that we would only be able to fish at night. There were no rules apart from common sense and to keep the venue and ourselves discrete, to which we all naturally agreed.

With no swims at all on the pit, just overgrown, reed-lined banks, a starting swim needed to be 'cut'. Before this was done I had been given a map of the lake, showing its contours and the unique 'obstacles' that were in its depths. Man-made snags shall we say – the likes of camper vans, taxis, a bus and a few other oddities to make it challenging. Something else that stood out was the lake's amazing clarity – it really is like tap water and you can often see the bottom in 20 feet of water!

A rare opportunity, but what lay ahead?

One of the prettiest carp I'll ever catch.

One thing that immediately struck me, reading the map, was the overall depth of the lake, averaging 25 feet. An early season start was out of the question because the water was incredibly cold due to the lake's natural underwater springs. Therefore, plans were made for a spring campaign.

I opted for the southwesterly corner of the pit, as not only would the carp arrive there when the warm winds came, it's also the shallowest end of the lake, coming out of the depths to a steady three metres in a small bay where the carp were known to spawn. At the very least I was hoping to see them in the bay at some stage.

Fishing Blind

I chose an area just in front of the mouth of the bay. In front of the swim there was a tall, thick reed bed. It was impossible to fish from the bank; my only way was to cut small channels in the reeds to poke the rods through. I kept these channels to a minimum so as to not draw too much attention to me. This, however, meant that I could also only fish while wearing waders. Plus, due to the height of the reeds I wasn't able to see the water and to a certain extent this meant that I was fishing blind.

I had a long, hard think about how I should approach the pit. As the fish had been reliant on natural food for the majority of their lives, plenty of prebaiting was needed. Sweetcorn was going to make up the majority of the feed – an instant attractor on any lake. However, I wanted to get the fish to accept other forms of food so I mixed the corn with pellet, hemp, tares and, slowly, boilies – Heathrow Bait Services' Indian Spice.

George, whose garden backs onto the

lake, fished the first evening back in April, while I continued to bait up. After a week or so baiting, George took several tench. He then fished the next evening and banked a common of 22lb, followed by a scale-perfect 31lb common. Due to my limited time, I decided to keep the bait going in throughout April and to then get the rod hours under my belt at the beginning of May. I tend to only fish one overnighter per week, but spend the rest of my time baiting the spots on early morning visits.

By my third night I was casting onto nice firm spots where carp had obviously been feeding. I choose to fish a corn/plastic corn combination on the rig at first, until I felt that they had accepted boilies as a food source.

Due to the depth, I fished small PVA mesh bags of crushed boilies and pellets, along with a nugget of dissolving foam around the hook and hair to keep it all in place until it settled on the spot.

That night I didn't hear any fish crashing and soon fell asleep. I was confident because I knew the fish had cleared the spots, but also knew it would be a waiting game. What I didn't know was when the carp were grazing the spot. They could've been feeding during the day and not at night! I couldn't believe my ears when, at 5am, my alarm signalled a blistering take. I jumped into my waders and ran down between the reeds to my rods. I stood there for a moment looking at the reel and, sure enough, the spool was spinning into a blur; an angry carp attached and putting distance between itself and me.

Secret Carp

Picking up the rod, I cupped the spool and leant into the fish. Steady pressure and tightening of the clutch slowed her down and I started to guide her back towards me. With no 'obstacles' in front of me, I knew I had nothing to worry about except the marginal reeds. As luck would have it, she stopped about six feet out from the reeds. I gained more line, until she kited back out into open water.

Finally, the black shape of my first secret carp popped up to the surface and was ready for the net. To my amazement and joy the fish wasn't a common - not that I'd complain if it had have been - but in fact a stunning mirror, which got the other lads and me very excited. Size was irrelevant, as she was beautiful and perfect. On the scales the needle read 27lb 10oz - I couldn't have asked for more, a true, yet rare fungus mirror lay in my arms. What a cracking way to start.

The baiting had to continue if I had any chance of keeping the fish visiting my spot and feeding regularly. Due to the times when we're allowed on the lake, my only option to bait is in the mornings before work. Living in Yateley and working in Guildford, the lake is hardly on the way and early starts are called for. I'd arrive at George's house around 6.30am, three times a week, launch the boat and set out to the area and bait the spots. I was usually all done by 7.30 and then it was off to work.

"Finally, the black shape of my first secret carp popped to the surface. It was not a common, but a stunning mirror."

Another Blank

The baiting continued every week and I started to ramp it up big style because I felt the big feeding time was approaching. For me, nothing had happened during June. July was soon upon us and I was due down one Friday night to find the swim was devoid of carp and another blank ensued. A couple of nights later, on the opposite bank, George banked another big common on HBS M&M boilies, that went 32lb plus. Encouraged by this, I started to introduce more boilies and fish at least one rod on them.

My next chance happened on my tenth

Back you go then.

A typically pristine Secret-Lake carp.

One of the original fungus mirrors.

night, this was at the beginning of July. I'd baited as per normal and decided to put two rods onto the spot where I'd had the mirror late in May. One rod was fished with corn, with two 14mm Indian Spice bottom baits on the other. The lines were slackened off and the bobbins set. Again the night was silent, and my sleep was once again interrupted at 5am by a single tone emanating from my buzzer. The boilie rod was away.

The fight was different to the mirror; this one was more angry and defiant, violently shaking its head. The only similarity was that it kited to my left along the reed line, but soon made its way back out into open water. Safely in the net first time, one of the lake's prized commons was mine. A 24lb 10oz, scale-perfect, bar of gold was held aloft for the waiting cameras. I only managed one more night in July, with nothing but a liner to show for it. The baiting continued though, but the lake had changed. I had been told that for a month of every year (usually the end of July) the crystal-clear waters suffered an algae bloom and turned a light green, which in turn slowed the fish to the point where they became quite lethargic.

I noticed a sudden abundance of naturals in the water. When I say abundance, I mean wading out to the rods, standing there for a few minutes and returning with 20 or so snails attached to my boots! It proved to be pointless fishing when the water was like this.

Time Out

I stopped baiting so often, and almost took a month off. In early August I had a week in America, and my plans were that, once I got home, the baiting would begin as before, and it did.

Tales from the owner led us to believe of sightings of a very large common. This has since been backed up by a couple of other people who have seen this particular fish in another corner of the lake sunning itself, including George. The first time I see it I want it to be in my net!

Another Secret-Lake carp kisses the block.

I returned to the lake mid-August and began the same baiting campaign. George hadn't fished the lake, as he knew that it was pointless while the water held colour. I fished a night at the end of August, but to no avail. George fished his swim and had a blistering take at 9pm. I wound in, clipped up and went round. We couldn't believe it; another big common had fallen to his rods – good angling. At 32lb 12oz it was also a new PB for George, so celebrations went ahead. After seeing another 30lb-plus common on the bank I was again all fired up for a return visit the following Friday night.

I baited early morning on the Monday and again on the Wednesday, with a total of 25kg of mixed hemp, corn, mini-tigers, pellets and boilies. I arrived quite late on the Friday, but luckily the light was still on my side and I was able to get the baits out on the spots. I was quite disappointed when I woke up at 6am and hadn't had a single bleep. I was sat up contemplating packing up early when my left-hand rod was away. Another angry common was attached and after steady pressure she succumbed to my efforts.

Proper Pleased

At 23lb 4oz I was proper pleased that another virgin common was being held up for the camera. I slipped her back into the depths and sat back to think for a minute. I'd fished this spot since May and had accumulated 20 nights for three fish, which I was happy with, as the lake is not easy at all. However, I felt something was wrong and that, although the bait was going in the same spot, the fish were really not coming down to that end of the lake in any great numbers and were only visiting for a bit of free grub. I had to move. It was a tough decision after all the bait and time I'd put in, and it did go through my mind that if I do move the fish would arrive etc, etc.

I wandered along the bank, just to the left of a marker buoy, and began to cut a new swim in the undergrowth and the reeds. According to the lake map, the buoy marks a submerged camper van. By this time it was mid-September and I was having to start the

The commons were fabulous...

... and the mirrors weren't bad either!

'I don't believe it exists'

THE BLACK MIRROR

'I've never seen it'

SHOULDERS

'There's no evidence to support it, only rumours'

ARFUR

'Not a trace, anywhere'

HEATHER

'Gardner PVA? Yeah, rite!'

MARY'S MATE

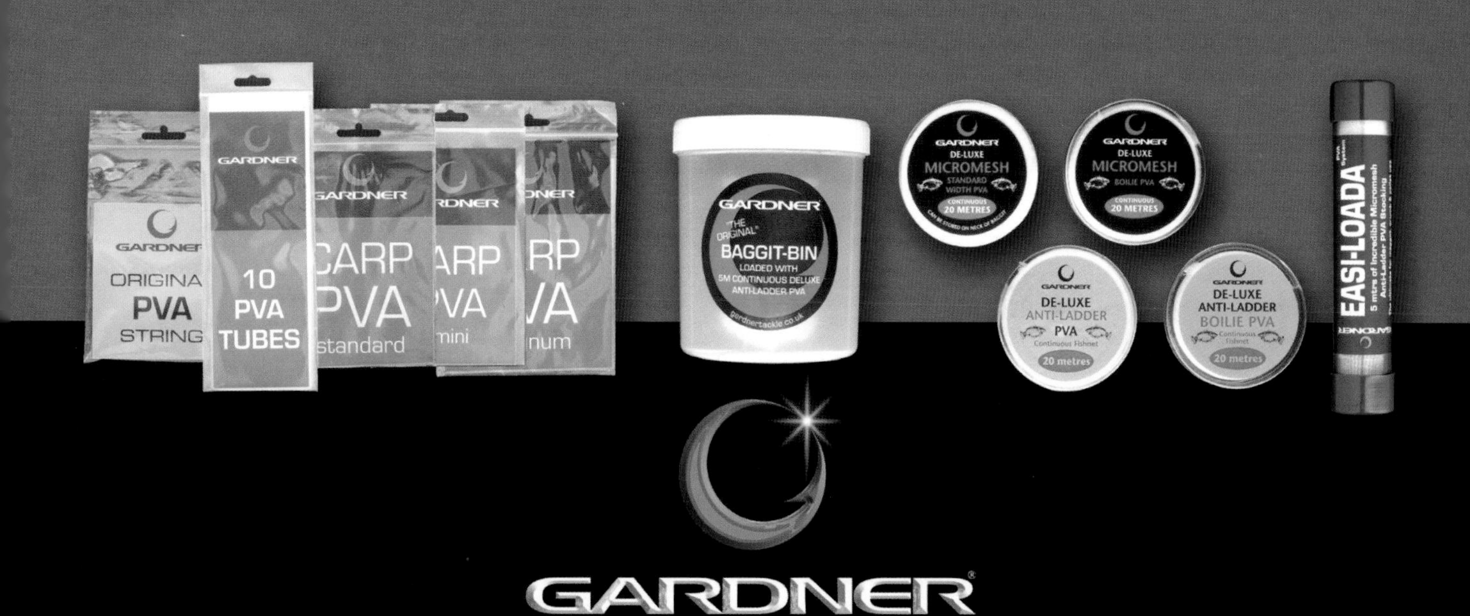

> I was on the phone to one of my mates when my left-hand rod ripped into life. I was straight into my waders and on it!

baiting once more – in an area that hadn't seen any bait yet. I decided to really put it in, upping the quantity to 25kg, twice a week, feeding only hemp, corn and a lot more boilies.

After a second week of baiting I felt it was the right time to fish the area. I arrived Friday evening after work and set about sorting out the rods and rigs: boilies-and-plastic-corn combination on one rod, boilies only on the middle and double tiger nut on the third.

I was on the phone to one of my mates at 9.15pm when my left-hand rod ripped into life. It scared the life out of me. I jumped straight into my waders and bent into a fish that was thankfully swimming in the opposite direction of the camper van! After a brief battle her head and shoulders broke the surface. I slid the net under her in the moonlight and a quick look revealed another well-built common.

Guest Session

The scales read 25lb 10oz this time – at least the commons were slowly getting bigger! A mate who was fishing the nearby lake kindly came over and did the honours with the camera, before I slipped her back. I put the rest of my bait in before leaving on the Saturday and returned to put some more in on the Tuesday. I also baited Thursday morning, which I was unsure about. I prefer to have two days between baiting and fishing the spot, but due to circumstances this couldn't be done this particular week. I arrived early on the Friday evening because I was meeting Mike Hutchinson (Cemex Fisheries manager), and I promised him a guest session on the lake. During the week I'd been thinking about the hook baits that I had got the bites on. Predominately, it was yellow baits that had produced most of the fish either corn/plastic or tiger nuts. I tinkered around with a rig that I hadn't used previously, one that my mate Garth Ethelston had shown me during some DVD filming a few weeks before. It was perfect for me to present a HBS Pineapple pop-up on, which I hoped would be a take-inducing alternative to what I had been fishing.

Rods out and ready for action.

I decided to put this rig on my middle rod and fish it between the other two, just for curiosity. Mike and I enjoyed a cracking Chinese and social and I retired back to base for a kip. I was awoken at 1.30am by a one-toner on the pop-up rod. I leant into the fish and was almost 'flat rodded'. Line was peeling off the spool, but again, thankfully in the opposite direction to the camper van. I eventually slowed the fish and in true style she started to kite. I gave Mike a shout, but didn't realise that he'd heard the take and was stood right behind me, which gave me a fright when he answered virtually in my ear! Once the fish tired I raised the rod up above my head, with the tip going back over my shoulder, and I brought her right up to the spreader block before I lifted the net.

I couldn't quite see in the moonlight and, excited as I was, I put my hand underneath her while she was in the net and gently lifted her up a bit so I could see my prize in the moon's rays. "Wow man, it's a big scaly mirror," I proclaimed! I passed the rod to Mike, while I collapsed the net and got her to the mat. We shone the torch on her and the light revealed the most stunning carp I had ever caught. Carefully, I unhooked her and placed her in the sling – 30lb 4oz. Very, very happy days! I packed up the next day and drove home with a huge grin on my face.

The weather had a distinct change in it the following week; temperatures were dropping, nights were drawing in and, for once, there was a steady barometric-pressure reading. I baited Tuesday and Thursday because I was due on the pit Saturday night. Over those two days a total of 50kg went out, but by Friday I didn't feel confident. I don't know why really. I had the same feeling

Saturday morning - something wasn't right. It was probably the easterly wind that was blowing, although my pitch was on the back of it. Anyway, I arrived at 3pm and started to set up my overnight camp, although I didn't cast until after 5.30pm. I put in 2kg of spod mix and then cast the baits out to the spots, all landing with a thud - which made me a bit more confident.

With the traps set, my mind was ticking away again. I hadn't fished over a biggish bed of bait during a session, so decided to put out the bucket, only 5kg in total, but it was different to the other times. While sat on my bedchair, I heard this boom as a gunshot rang out behind me. There's nothing unusual about that down there - rabbit hunters. It happened again, this time it sounded too close. It did make me jump - and think! Next thing I know the fall-out shot is splattering off my brolly! Thankfully that was all; perhaps the rabbits had moved on quite a bit! Proper close for my liking though! With the shooting over and my nerves settled I got my head down.

> **"I'd remembered my torch this time and I was shocked again when I turned it on to see the scale pattern of a chunky linear – top result!"**

Steady Take

At 11.30pm I woke to a steady take on my left-hand rod. I hit the take and almost stopped the fish. I could feel the violent head shakes as it kited to the reed line. She stayed a long way down the reeds before stubbornly letting herself be lead back towards me. Every now and then we had a stalemate and she'd hit the surface, thrash about and then dive deep again. Eventually, I dipped the net under her and lifted. Another jewel was mine.

I'd remembered my torch this time and I was shocked again when I turned it on and saw the scale pattern of a chunky linear - top result. The scales read 25lb 12oz, and in the sack she rested in preparation of the morning photo shoot. Matt kindly made his way over from the nearby lake to take the pics. Just before he arrived my middle rod burst into life, again much to my surprise, and a very powerful fight ensued. I bent into the fish that immediately took loads of line, this time it did flat-rod me. With steady pressure I

Well pleased!

started to feel the line grate through what I thought was weed. As much as I tried, although I managed to stop and gain some kind of control over the fish, the line continued to grate through until… the rod sprang back at me as the line parted on the mussels that festoon the weed! I was absolutely gutted. Deep down I think I'd just lost one of the big girls. The fish felt so powerful compared to the 25-pounder the night before. Matt arrived and my attentions turned to the sacked fish. In the morning light it looked stunning and I have to say that I'm very grateful for that beautiful linear. It was the perfect end to the season, unlike the chickenpox that brought that end somewhat prematurely. But, like they say in the movies, I'll be back…

Sadly, sunrise meant home time.